Customary
Etiquettes

Customary
Etiquettes

Bèrj A. Terjimanian

Library of Congress Control Number:		2020914582
ISBN:	Hardcover	978-1-6641-2255-0
	Softcover	978-1-6641-2256-7
	eBook	978-1-6641-2254-3

Print information available on the last page.

Rev. date: 08/27/2020

To order additional copies of this book, contact:
Xlibris
844-714-8691
www.Xlibris.com
Orders@Xlibris.com
784524

CONTENTS

To my loved ones in Spirit: my beloved parents, Assadour and Arshaluyce; my two brothers, Jacob and Big John; my sister Vicky; and my uncle Hagop

Acknowledgements

I greatly admire the contributions of the following people: Mr. Haroutiun Keoroghlanian of Sydney, Australia, for being my mentor and for giving me help in writing poems in English; Miss Helen Hartman of Oregon, who acted as a sounding board for improving the poems I wrote in the 1980s; and Ms. Judi Messina of Houston, Texas, who not only typed the manuscript but also indirectly shaped this book artistically.

BOOK I

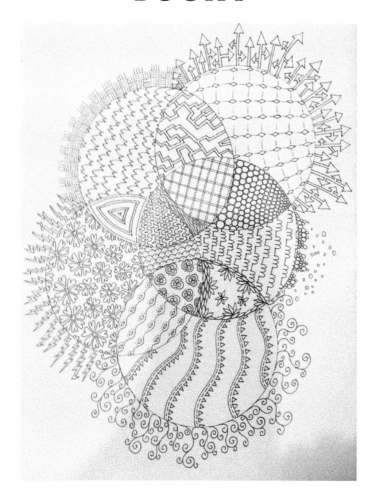

...Opus '67

BOOK I

OPUS '67

Echo-Contrast Poems

Poems written before 1968

PERIPHERIES OF CONVOLUTED THOUGHT PROCESSES

(a) **Perimeter of Integrity**

what is so dense
not incense
not of lead as
what my love has

in you, my dense

cluster
of atoms of perpetualness

(b) **Efficacies of a Telltale Heart**

humanity:
acceding
receding
on the tomb
snowing

angel:
crying
her tears
s n o w i f y i n g

eventually:
(the trend)

life,
living,
moving,
will end.

(c) **I Will Tell**

life is too long
to make it song

(d) **Heed**

a cat in fury
may be a Tory

(e) **Trepidation**

my heart speaks softly
if there is love within ye
and if I can love — will
she not render her love to me?

(f) **A Moment's Glance**

a moment's glance
not in trance
or disbelief
at her,
can commotion spur

a moment's glance
all doubts prance
at me
yet she — tranquil,
calm, sad —
Ilsabil

(g) **Astonishment**

I could draw
yon pale crow
on my elbow
with lipstick

(h) **Oversized Stone**

my cat thinks of nothing but mischief
he has made a respectable reputation as a thief

my love thinks of nothing but antipathy
but I shall still love her by means of telepathy

my house is a prison for me from now on
I still believe the moon to be an oversized stone

my soul torments me like a mallet on my ribs
wanting to flee my earthen body, it reduces me and
further nips

(i) **Quivering Tigris**

when the shadow of your smile
meets the quivering Tigris,
then Melancholia (with a guile)
will penetrate into your iris

(j) **1968**

in this Night Prowler–ian atmosphere,
my sweet Ida, have no fear

(k) **Pictures**

a fish in a fish's belly
in my heart my sweet Ahnee
a cotton machine by Tweedales & Smalley

a mouse in a cat's stomach
a bison chewing spinach
my robot driving a Cadillac

(l) **Poet Sad**

poet sad, you are unwise
to talk of things un-po-e-tic
(to go lamenting for no catch).

(m) **Intimate Bird**

I.

the peak of the Air endures a broken heart:
'tis the Bird — it feels so far away from Man
I fancy to wear her Garment and start
postulations that Man is so wan
and unstill. oh, to feel the Bird inside
and sweep unerringly in Ether and ride

II.

to screen all the unpremeditated glory
of the haughty plains and be lit
and *leaping* in the heart and really
understand how mode anew it is

(n) **Solar Motives**

the poetry of Earth is never read
by Poets alone,

but also by scientists, teenagers, politicians,
and liberated women.

(o) **Dreams**

    dreams are made of
alabaster
tissue fiber
the soul and psyche
the river Tiber
exports of the cerebrum

(p) **Philosophy of Propensity**

    to keep a clear head
is like being wed
to Supreme Sobriety

(the Daughter of Gladness, i.e.)

Tappy, How Do You Write A Poem?

sit down … I will explain.
use a rich-flowing pen — one that's been healed
in soft metaphors.
do not sit rigid. express
your intent and don't smudge your content,
be live-wired,
yet do not become entangled
in the season's habitual tenors.
face the class if you envision yourself as a
commentator/teacher
and be bold about your decree
and carriage.
if you are climbing, don't fall
or leap down high stories or mountains.
maintain safety and a sense of mission.
use the right torque of pressure, be
an elevated Michelangelo — be
a governor/manager.
beware of letting your tutorship grow
beyond conducive matriculation.
focus and compute: don't be rash like Scaramouch
or fearless like Cyrano,
but defend your principles.
stand your ground and —
declare an Anticipation Commission.

A Summer Rain

is one that washes
 the dust from the plain
 and
extinguishes hot, parched squares.

I don't fear the clouds
 or the thunder
 or the lightning.

note, you, this is the morning after;
this poem is the continuation of its self.
this poem is a reaching-out poem,
 for its evolution,
destiny, dexterity,
prismaticism, personhood.

so in a way,
 this is a remark unto attic.
 this is
an essay for display and rhetoric.
 this is …
express-and-confess-but-hide-the-reasons
kind of play.

* * *

 the highest picture in my mind's eye
is one of the migrating birds:
 eurythmic creatures journeying
 on a single road,
 going straight, evincing a clear diagram

on a brisk, determined heaven
full of sun protein (as much as vials),
                   of tone, merit, grace, luminosity,
                      blandishment, and geniality.
these winged sentries have crossed the Chersonese
     and departed the loam of the Delta.
they have climbed over the white horses of the Main
     and circumscribed the chiromancy of the hobbledehoy
                                   cadet.

ah, sunset approaches.
     the clouds are still rosy in their pigmentation.

Heart has released its tendrils and breathes the air
     in the perfume of the orchard.
Breeze gets stronger, temperature milder, respiration
                          easier.

hints of quietude nestling;
restitude leafing; energy regenerating, building,
                         fluxing.

The Man on the Train

I saw him sitting in his usual seat,
his eyes closed and face folded,
not in nap or thought,
but in veneers of softness and quiet.

The softness is most noticeable in
the quality of his face: a quiet
assurance, an integrity,
an unlimited reservoir of kindness,
a sea of harmony, mock aloofness.

Formfitting, you are what you wear
and how you stand, how you true
your tie to grooming standards,
a speck of dust one too many
if it is in the wrong place…

Like snippets from movies,
the train offers glimpses
of the changing vista outside
through its windows,
iron wheels, metal bars securing the plain…

Blending of White and Blue

owh,
    tell me 'bout
ahboot (HOOT! MANN!
      HOOT! MANN!)

    ohtellme'boutth'

       blending of white and blue
(navy blue, snow white)
  (police blue, taffeta white)
    (velvet blue, cream white)
      (sky blue, terrace white).

A Penguin

A penguin on the shore
is one that I adore.

Crests and Troughs

I wander, sullen, in dull evening, away,
wonder and shout, slinging a voice in the sway
of the murky waters gray, longing to carry me,
in their tress-laps into olden memory.

I imagine the craft, a beautiful picture lulling cold,
and the horizon pitless, meek and lost
in moss gray; the scouts' corpses of torches aflare,
ducking restlessly into a wombish snare.

I forgot all things about me and fell,
and dozed along this great spell.

now,
the crimson scarves of the summit did lamp,
on wild nature's moors the Rays made camp,
and I palely awaited the cuckoo to stamp

me with a trillion wishes amp.

Prose Poem Entitled "Vokébar"*

           ... yes,
you were saying how the girl next door looked more
beautiful than you, and the stars in such nice array, only —
you wouldn't comply with all that complaining Beethoven
and a little more champagne than in last night's
dream, speaking to yourself in a manner so provoking as
that. Ah, how marvelous to be kissing in such a polite
way so as not to ruin the paint, walking very ladylike and
with high strides, with a cigarette in your fingers, chuckling at
life and at yourself. Nourished by the thought of a grasshopper
through the fields and with the light rain bringing
memories of the happy and sad hours, you sat by the lamp,
looking expectantly interested in the spark of a thought
of a dream of A and A and A and a final materialism.

           ... you
were telling me the story of your eyes, how once they
saw and measured differently, and the colors were interpreted
differently in each dimension; but it was when they loved
each other and soon married that you were able to see
things as one, without the soul overstepping the individual.
Ah, but as they married, they simultaneously killed their
love due to its excess and dissolved it in itself. In regard
to its by-product, that third eye of the subconscious was
like a sun that lit the path toward infinity.

           ... then
you were talking of the tragedy of your ears, how the
one would hear the whispers of the angels and the curt pluck
of the harp and the sound created by the communication
between two naiads and the muffled sad tune trapped between
two hearts pleading to each other.

lastly, the sore palpitating music of time, so unnerving, recurring, invigorating, yet silent voice yet hollow voice of the, of the, of the, of the, and the and oh! the *strange rhythm of its twist!*

* *Vokébar* means "dance of the spirit" in Armenian.

Stone, Campfire...

… and walrus are what I need now.
A stone with a rough face.
Campfire that permeates the skin.
Walrus of stout ambition and ivory stare …

… the burial of silver, spires, turrets,
lithe costumes adorning pixieish partygoers.
Plumes of smoke and blankets of fronds.

Let Streams Coat

your discriminating interests
let powers remote
                    hem, re-
fashion
        the tarp epaulettes;
nuclear threats,
                        let mingle
and disappear
        into the crowds of opposing protesters.

let them be hammered
        with red nails
        yellow chagrin
and purple resolve
        into the very ribs
        of the Atlantic Ocean.

let dreams, new, fresh, bright,
        extricate man from his wounds;
let love flow, expand, yell
and claim herself
        a new
                con-ti-nent.

Found in an Aulde Booke

"Nyethere wine noir thy keisses,
Wilt intoacxicaet me with deasyre;
Minde ye! Naethynge ofte worths ane earth wilt laeste!
Aenn' soone, a' paewere aenn' love wilt expire … !"

Rebecca*

wind and aroma
of warm coffee;
fed by insomnia,
chocolate, toffee.

music from a radio.
nuns' hymns struggling to be heard.
D'Artagnan saying "Adieu,"
spending hours on one word.

I, trying to forget her face,
the blue ribbon in her hair;
throwing in fancy an ace,
cigarette butts everywhere.

* one of my "immature" poems, written at age seventeen

Death

men yet will come,
men yet will go;
but on the tomb,
it will snow.

but in the end,
all men will die!
that's the trend;
do not cry!

no angel cried,
but her tears
snowified
over the years.

A Love History

I.

She rose like a dancing fire,
Amidst the vivid colors of spring;
And as the sun's might expired,
Her sole aim and care was to sing.
But an angel at moon's downfall
Came and stole her from me! Stole!

The sole treasure that I possessed!
Her voice I did hear no more!
The color of her eyes I expressed,
In my sorrow abundant with lore!
But an angel at moon's downfall,
Came and stole her from me! Stole,

The very essence of her innocent face;
Her soft mien crimsoned in pink fire;
Her gentle arms, which I wanted to embrace;
And the particular blend of her attire!
Ah, an angel at moon's downfall,
Came and stole her from me! Alas!

II.

Three hundred years have passed.
I have shed tears, which 'fore tears increased.
I have hollowed my eyes, made my face aghast,
And now the weeping has stopped, the heartache ceased.
Strew wind and rain, petals and spears,
O ye angels high, in your evanescent spheres!

Sensitive hearts everywhere, stop, feel and listen!
Notice the valor in my heart, the integrity in my breast.
See the scope of my love, which vibrates messages written
In the deeper chapters of my life, O friends who are my guest!
Strew wind and rain, romance and rhapsody,
O ye angels high, breathing joy and harmony.

Angels, angels, a flutter of lips, my prayer is to thee!
My yearning and desire, my will for eternity!
Smooth the shores where pebbles as sharp as glass
Might cut other lovers' feet as they climb the pass.
Strewn with wind and rain, with flowers and songs and pins,
Might angels high heal Ozymandias neath the ruins.

*Verb Castles**

(Yesterday a Lemon Tree)

Time murmurs carry me
Over gray walls on rooftops
Cold, pungent gale bistros and …
Parading slivers of mutant sun-pulp

Ladders, flowerpots, catnooks, rare-appearance
Vagaries and staunch trees;
Enthusiastic visitors, partakers, brief
And long and convex-concave friends.

You and I have a thing or two,
A blue chill, a cough, a sneeze, a pest!
We shudder, debrace, constrict, beglue,
At times acting out behaviors we detest!

Let us forgive and cancel our petty debts,
By endeavoring to live by newer and larger thoughts.

Now a lot of ideas
And thoughts
Are roller-skating
Between the late-afternoon
Rays that are themselves
Pungent and glowing in orange
And best character

The clouds
Are getting thinner
As the drops of moisture

From treetops and brambles
Fall onto cheeks and dashing eyebrows,
Tall, zany hats, and low, low necklines.

I'll be leaving my home at night
To walk over the crumpled city
To inhale persimmon windows
To listen to solitary radio beacons
To listen to un-curfewed insects.

Dimly lit tables will be my forte, sparse intelligences
Tolerated for the comforts of a spy's rewards

Ah, how marvelous to be kissing in such a polite way
So as not to ruin the paint
Walking very ladylike and with high strides
With a cigarette in your fingers
Chuckling at life and at yourself
I wander, sullen, in evening, away
Wonder and shout, slinging a voice in the sway
Of the murky waters gray, longing to carry me,
In their tress-laps into olden memory.

And the summer rain
Is one that washes
The dust from the plain and
Extinguishes hot, parched squares
I don't fear the clouds or the thunder or the lightning
Note, you,
This is the morning after,
This is a continuation of its self
This is a reaching-out poem—for its evolution
Prismaticism, and personhood.

So in a way,
This is a remark unto attic.
This is
An essay for display and rhetoric;
This is
An express-and-confess-but-hide-the-reasons kind of play.

* "Verb Castles" is a *pastiche* poem, a French form combining several poems.

There is A Faint Voice

There is a faint voice; it is of John Keats.
Which, with its lyre, my soul greets;
Where death shall no more cheat,
While our warm hearts continue to beat.

There is a name in that note,
Which is somehow held in the throat;
The birds use it, and all the trees,
Are informed through the breeze.

While our tears shall form a fountain,
And water the buds on the mountain;
While that voice shall cease to be weak,
On its high glittering peak.

It shall be a bud greener and smacked,
By a tip of purple and by mirth be cracked;
And open its heart and the high atmosphere smell,
While the tips of the lyre shall say "Farewell!"

Establishment

I could escrow
in dialect
resilient as a bow
with tongue in cheek
'n' tow.

John

why did you give up your dream?
astute you were; I looked up to you.
gentle, smiling, kind, debonair with the ladies;
what would take me weeks, sometimes months,
to clench up my courage to speak to them, you did fluently,
almost effortlessly. I should know, of course (with
a secret grin tucked in those dimples of yours!),
gregarious you were, as if people, from the pope
down to the cobbler, the tailor, and the scoutmaster,
were more approachable than a deity or the fleet
of the Spanish Armada.
you certainly were more spontaneous, with a lot more
courage next to your handkerchief in your breast pocket.
John, why did you give up your dream?

Tale of the Poetess

I.

the poetess rose,
she ate a rose,
then a rose more,
till it digested in her core.
she hoped that
neither frog nor cat
would see her
rising songs stir.
this it was —
she craved, this lass,
for some inspiration;
the rose gave her indigestion!
she squelched in indignation!
she wrought her tears
in a cauldron of bitter-flowing sounds.

in her straw hat then,
she found her pen.

II.

in a cold mind,
she scanned the pond,
which reverberated
with free-flowing
plume arrows.
wrapped in bedsheets,
her face was near freezing.

III.

the water
gift-boxed her eyes
and tossed them back to her.
she, half asleep,
thinking
of warm garments,
a fire, a bed,
finally got up,
threw the deepest sigh
from her shivering chest,
and uttered the iciest groan,
astounding
the nocturnal insects,
rubbing her pink-and-blue lips
with a patch
of her evening dress.

IV.

tulips
her hands:
that's how she folded them.
sky-blue sheets
she unravelled,
placing the floweriness
of her soul
in that firm cot.
perfume
emanated
from the windowsill.

she sleeps now,
an elvish pulse,

papery whispers
of night stars,
beige comets.

she sleeps now,
unwrinkled,
amaryllis.

BOOK II

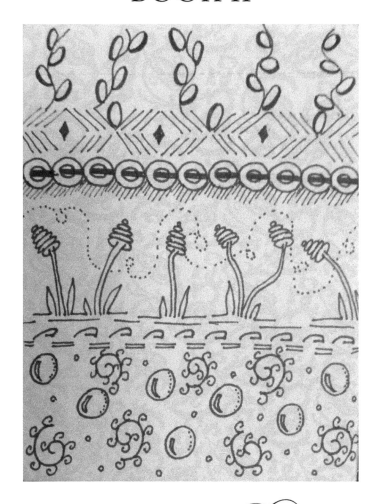

...Burrowing Shale Poems

BOOK II

BURROWING SHALE POEMS

Burrowing Shale

A POEM-STORY

Burrowing Shale Poems
A human-history saga
recounted through
a sheaf of passages

A fantasy story
set in poetry

BY WAY OF EXPLANATION

Burrowing Shale Poems is a collection of poems that tell a story. Although some of these individual poems may seem disjointed or not related to the main theme, in a real sense they actually are.

A lot of the sequences, especially of a stream-of-consciousness mood, have been placed there in order to facilitate a memory recall for both the author and mass (race) consciousness.

Fragments and visions that come to the author in poetic form are simply the points and facets that he is aware of.

ONE

Water from Wales

(Prose poem with intentional built-in rhyme)

Water from Wales … *I bought water from Wales* … just imagine … crisp, clear water in a blue bottle, called *Still*; I think it means very still … so that when you drink it, it won't rush toward your palate like champagne or plaster you like Madeira from Spain … It won't intoxicate you quickly like Athens's *ouzo* or dull your senses like tap water.

I drank it; it tasted good. It went very well, following food. I wonder how … my tastes will vary when … well, when I marry … (but this may not happen in Wales, only … in *Twice-Told Tales*.)

Alas … the actor with the goatee stood on his haunches, so see? The period picture was exacting, I know, I feel that they weren't all acting … but then … they, uh, probably … didn't know about Welsh water … *(and certainly nothing about your daughter).*

TWO
A World Away
(With short built-in rhyme, unintentionally placed)

She listened beneath eight hundred miles of sandstone, ice, and shale. Her home was made of nature's bric-a-brac, whatsoever she could find or rummage, including naturally occurring quartz, pink duff stone, and other smooth pieces honed by nature over time and made tolerably smooth and feminine with awkward tools that she also had to make or improvise.

I pinned a poem to one of her antechambers, connected by stalactites and the remains of creatures that resembled the stegosaurus and the woolly mammoth. There were some subterranean forms of life that had apparently survived and that were tapping the damp crevices of water or seeking warmer regions. I found these smaller bipeds and anthropoids by tapping at a small sapling at my end, eight hundred miles away. And when she did finally hear me from that distance, she hummed a tune of silver tines and gold forks. This vibration excited and teased the molten lead of Mount Etna into wanting to, but not erupting.

All this transpired, unfortunately, to the beating of the lizards' hearts. They were disturbed out of their warm cottony beds and waited on the nearby peninsula, watching the traffic of terns go by.

But as I said earlier, I was a world … away *(sigh)* and none the wiser.

The pool shimmered over the frosted frigid skirts of alfalfa, lichen, and birch blossoms blown from far-flung areas, populating *their* kingdoms.

SHALE

no. 17

Waves crashing. And I hear the distinct cry of the loon as it searches for its partner in the vastness. Our eyes meet. The sea rages.

Jagged teeth of the cliffs. How they chew the sea. Primordial vapor—
first course soup: *potâge**
with
bread … For bird and beast alike.

The bell tolls. The town square is quiet. Bundled in shawls and rosemary essence, the women
look
pure. Their red-brown cheeks match their painted lips.

The men are rough, subdued. Under their Sunday best, you can see them pursing their eyes under
the
unwanted weight of pressed white shirts and scented jackets. Their gnarled hands pull with a stiff yearning apparent in the fluxing of the overhanging tree.

They *both* seem rooted in their spots …

* French, for "soup"

SHALE

no. 18

I yearn for freedom.
For myself and all others.
For captors and captured.
For all elephants under yoke.
For rajahs and maharajahs who torture those elephants.
For masters and mistresses who own power over others.
For princes and princesses who *think* they own.
For jailers and captives suffering from hardness.
For satellites and moons that are under rule of planets.

For kings and queens with too many to-dos under their crowns.
For sheep and cattle who are not aware of their troubles.
For all gnomes who punish.
For all elves who are punished.

For gods and demigods.
For gurus and monks.
For you.

SHALE

no. 19

The rain came. She remained embraced to the trunk of the tall palm, its fronds flailing wildly from the wind. Like an elephant sheltering her young, the perennial stood assiduously while the island *screamed* under the cane of the storm.

The island was a copper penny, or it was a shilling, or a large pebble in a basin. Its fronds to the east took the brunt of the storm, their tresses opening to the tooth of a comb. And the banshee, master barber, groomed each one of them daintily.

The beaches remained a pan-trough for this seemingly hungry dog who was lapping the water feverishly. The sand-tarts commune, *"The rain ends, so soon?"*

A trombone announces, *"Intermissionly"*.

SHALE

no. 20

In the muted laughter, the air had freshened and softened, as soft as her eyebrows in that tethered tent.

He had collected her, as one collects wild honey and jasmine, in his *oh-so-manly* arms, that she'd *fainted*. Drowsy in dreams, delirious from starvation, she had clung to life, her lungs doing breaststrokes on a serene lake.

It was not only romance but friendship and laughter — that was this new wine in old cups which had made her sick.

Upon awakening, she told her dreaming mind, she would discard the wine and drink fresh from the stream …

SHALE

no. 21

She lives in the world inside our world, which itself sits snugly in another, almost like a cup-in-a-cup,
fitted together as smoothly as a ship's hull.

She tends a small garden, among which some of the flowers are dying and others have grown pale due to neglect. Her home is her garden, and the cyclops is heaving his shoulders against the naked face of the mountain to annoy her.

She speaks, but I pretend not to hear.

I commune, but the rumble from the shaggy giant's ministrations drowns out my voice.

Finally, after torturous hours, her hair, now brittle and caramelized by fear, breaks like a shroud
of glass in a cathedral spire in a city called Rome.

BOOK III

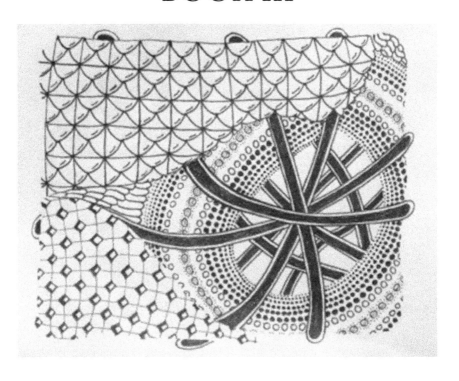

... Jazz Poems

JAZZ I

CLASSIC JAZZ

Kaleidoscope Poem

I.

Yellow and maroon leaves
dry
     dim
          crisp
living with these stones
who are lonely too.

Pastel,
     artsy,
          so *Miro,*

these leaves sigh
when addressed;
most of them await

The Second Coming
          of the Wind.

II.

the reddish ones —

                vermilion
                bricky
                flame

                claim

a nobler heritage.
in better days
they swayed with taffeta skirts
in rich manners

their brothers
came from aristocracies;

their sisters used to shade
fellow women sitting in garden chairs
in those old Italian mansions;
cloying those elegantly dressed,
                delicately perfumed,
                ravishing chambermaids …

How You

tap and dance,
          how you
move around, turn things over,
          kick
tin cans in
          tin-can alleys
(tin storefront alleys)

          & how
you use energy freely, letting it run playfully
          through your hands
just like on the beach
          on the coral shelf
     (in the Pacific)
          & how
you lean your elbows against the wall
          to lean
     or keep from slipping … or invite
a hippo in your arms with a happy approach …

          well, we'll continue that later; you know?
oh, et cetera.

Net of Hearts, Scout Revelries

naked girl
before naked sea
at dusk

hair nucleus spine
tows a mollusk
knees in thought

mind; her whole
body thinks
waves give and take

so very still,
I would think
she sprung from that clove of cliffs.

Note

Leif, on the painting, I'd like
        Por's expression of satiety,
            Tara's intimate poise and gaiety,
and still life; within
        the tent a reed-lantern,
           bed with brass frame,
              expound nature, draw
multifarious cascades … engaging atmosphere.
        complete it by Friday …

p.s.: also puma, Hevelutta Hexiroyce.

There is A Certain

quiet in the air,
a quiet I cannot compare
                    to anything
heretofore, or after.
Oh, see …
    even the ladder is down
flat, on its face;
even the chambers are drawn

and   the mule is meek
                        it's
        fast asleep

and   the teardrop's frozen
                    on the face of
        that wayward child

and   the door on the lattice
                        has
        not been unlatched

by   any intruder
                    or
        known person.

Petty Peeves

I'll be leaving my home at night
to walk over the crumpled city,
to inhale persimmon windows,
to listen to solitary radio beacons,
to listen to uncurfewed insects.

one, I will run to a social scientist;
query him, bombard him with subatomic issues.

two, I will run in profuse sweat and pound
on the gates of a convent, in the hope that

a stratifying fear will emanate from the chambers
within, and fearsome and angry authorities

will rebuke, repudiate, scathe; ominous cats
will be awakened … I may even be fortunate

to be considered
progenitor of classified lectures, monitor of informations.

dimly lit tables will be my forte'; sparse intelligences
tolerated for the comforts of a spy's rewards …

Reverie

(First version)

I am at the seashore
I am holding a camera
I am taking photographs
I don't know what for.

I hear whispers and cries
I see people from afar
I observe them swimming
I sense my own surprise.

I huddle when the wind blows
I shiver as the sun sets
I bury my knees in the sand
I cover myself in blankets.

I shiver and scrawl on
the dingy, tattered white page,
I mutter something, oh I don't know,
something about the sun being
very pale and beige …

Reverie
(Second version)

I am at the seashore
I am holding a camera
I am taking photographs
I don't know what for

I hear whispers and cries
I see sea gulls flying by
I feel the scene must be one
In which nothing is quite still

I see people from afar
So far they look like spider-mites
I observe them swimming
I sense my own surprise

I run over a ditch that's frozen stiff
Over spots as thin as hungry beaks
I press the horizon to contravene
Weakness in my feet and sense of peace

I huddle as the wind blows
I shiver as the sun sets
I bury my knees in the sand
I cover myself with blankets

I scrawl wave sand memory
With dingy fingers in my notebook
I drink ocean I listen clear
For new echoes fresh hemispheres …

If Poetry is Your Weakness

__+__

If poetry is your weakness,
Then, examine this book and its thickness;
Quite a volume! AD 2059 edition!
Rose-cloth bound, in excellent condition!

Pillow on A Sea

I am continually amazed
at
the

dots
and
dashes   lines
                and
clusters   splashes
and
flasks   tonic
                hatches
vigor
and
entelechy   parures
                and

waves   seals

and

bathyscopes   boats

               and

coats   islands

and

timepieces.   boys

               and

               girls

Constraint

let a corner of your eye
be sufficiently buried,
and twining collect
the thigh and
posture
and self,
and
let
remarkability
adjust its
triangle of conclusion
after the Council
has convened,
then
strike a conversation
after observation,
and complete your arc
of reflection.

Description

gray and rain-interspersed wind.
>> not cold, not hot, oft bright, oft dark,
a mixture of moods,
>> not Arab, not Hind',
not going, not coming, not moving, not
>>>> an Ark …

not awake, not sleeping,
>> but gathering wheat for thought,
not listening, not conversing,
>> not looking at faces, yet,
not cracking, not moulding,
>> sand castles/clay boat,
not expressing, not hoarding,
>> queries, or conclusions, Pet!

this is not a spume of clouds,
>> nor a catch of robins' nests.
this is not a heated tort,
>> nor a voluminous protest.
neither is it a hostelry of conquerables,
>>>> or bettor bests,

ah, in no way take it my dear,
to mean a periscope-y of jests!

Did You Drink

did you drink
that flask of ink?
because you look
Lemurian pink!

Yeti

I am astounded at the height
where silver grows fastest

> in strands through
> forays

> above incurious

s
  a
    u   when   aphonic,
   r   nights,   purling,
  i
 a
n   envelope
  s   the husk and shivering membranes

of the stellar fronds.

Time Capsule

        hello,

hello =   +hello

    hello! hello!

..........................h............i!!!!!

    perhaps you are one/

perhaps

thousands in one

perhaps/ a thousand

subleaders of all

    but none

in … sometimes

our knowing future/ or your

towing past. this/ our arm extension

to/…???

…our concern is

not to teach the good/

or the bad …but … at our suggestions,

keep: music

    telegraph poles

    fossil museums

1965 Chantilly

discard: the mantle shell

Twenty-Third-Century Shopper

in an overall abortive study
of my shopping adventure today,
one would link
escalator penguin-strokes
of decorated, pensioned, persevered
iron follicle of substance-trait vitality
to a good night's wink
she flirts her nails on cameo-beige knapsacks
a green-mascaraed lady —
among the shuffle, moisting
                     her lips with indigo;
I touch blue spheres, alloy gowns
coarse knee-scarves, broad hats
I sit
      in the center of that vein
watch hearts enclasped with darting eyes
even when they seem too involved and not seeing
transfixed and caught in these prickly nettles
and feel a warmth despite the
                     shivering radiation
that ensues from pulsating dynamic mast-cloistered lady B-52s
(Motto on the wing decrees: Marauding Aims)

Sand Stirring into Ocean

it is a balmy, patriarchal evening.
outside, it is nothing and void.
dark and dank, artificial gladness,
she sits in the nook, her mind paranoid.

scamp humorists, bilious priestly piers,
drenched whirlpools of plastic faces;
she is sole skipper of her flaccid fears
she dissolves pell-mell, irresolute, in paces.

Describe to Me, The Myuuuuuhhzeeekkkkkk!!!!!!!!

it wells up,
it's not sad, but eye-broken,
less tearful, more hugging-oneself.

you can
close your self and acquiesce the pools
in which

limelights
and trepid, slender bachelor girls
lounge

slovenly.

Soon, People

Soon, people will become quiet.
they will spring their arms
                        and throw a priv.*
Shaking bites out of their course of vision
as they hold their glance in equitable pander,
with their milk-and-tart.

* privilege

Antimony of Faraday

where there is night
I often immerse
in the moonbeam bright,
to roll forth some verse.

salient prisms
cherish that light
in the cool universe.

telepathic winds,
(they carry it.)

where share we the height
a prestige badge, —
sparkling notch, in the cool universe
cool universe
cool universe
cool universe
cool universe
cool universe
cool universe

Measured Ambition

If the world were a copper canyon and I but its sole survivor,
I would take the L train to see all its shiny surfaces,
corrugated turrets,
goosenecks
                    of its tea services.

If the world were a clay model, I would press it into vanilla beans
                    slender; with dance-like steps,
AWE-ditioning to Nazi audiences: opera in a castle, dour gazes,
chairs, balconies as correct as … political(ly).

If the world were a school for ballet,
I would measure its students' feet like spouts in a granary
                    endlessly pouring flour into bottomless
sills, moulding their ankles in symphony.

If the world were fay and everybody were wearing
                    a pin-striped suit and had jet-black hair
and sauntered brilliantly, like men and women with purpose.

If Night met Day
                    in choreographic behavior,
and courted like a jester in a Will's play,
blushing copiously to the applause of millions …

If, like ventriloquists of puppet-plays,
Time wooed Beautiful Girl, and her passionate heart swelled
on her rising breast, Oh just a small dinghy marooned in storm,
breaking in form, listing her knee … (dammit …)

If Measured Ambition
                snatches me into this perilous journey;
duets, Alpert, Tijuana Brass, Sargasso,
artful chimes, Hovaness,
                Beowulf, clarinet, duduk,
Apollo, Diana,
                Thrace …

                core and spittle
                music from Source
           coned paws, chipmunks, Satyrs embrace,
Marionette, Deva, Angel, Sugar, Plum-my-buttercup-Wings,
Ambitions on stage, opera, decibels with fluid female anatomies …

Are you breathing?

Sunlight

sunlight on the ginger jar *lamp*
          falls   *mar*
     through the mini-blinds
                   king

     pppattternnnss
S   ttt H slices A*rivets*   R   D   S
     pa   e
    p   r
    p   nnnss
M s E   tic T sig   A *nets*
    u   s
     rr. i
     eal
sunlight being blocked by *this*
        enclo   sure
   I've just described
                creates

   ssstrrrangggee
     rrr
S   st a HA swelling   DO   W   S
    s   n
    s   gggee
TO p   ingerlamp THE WALL
    as   g
     tthe
SUNlight, I am about to go to sleep
        now   *rece*
   do your expending and
              ding

ascloūuuddsss

     uuu

AND   gently bump *you*   YOU

       o   d

T   cl W dsss   I   T   C   H,

  I

     to   st go, and do my *thing*

       omu

SUNlight, when the afternoon *comes,*

       please

     wake me and then   *un*

             leash

     allofyourpower

AS   www   HARD   AS   you   wish

    po   e

   p   r

B   b   U   e the TT on all O those N sha S dows

   u   h

    r   t

    sting

Sun-Light

sun-light on the ginger-jar lamp,
falls through the mini-blinds;
marking patterns, slices, rivets,
shards, *meta-surrealistic* signets.

sun-light, being blocked by this —
enclosure I've just described,
creates strange swelling shadows
past the ginger-jar lamp, to the wall.

Sun-Light, I am about to go to sleep;
now, do Your expanding and receding —
as clouds gently bump You, and You
twitch, I too must go and do my *thang!*

Sun-Light, when the afternoon comes,
please wake me, and then unleash
all Your power, hard as You wish!
burst the buttons on those shadows!

Sun-Light, being amused by this,
intimate morning tryst,
softly rocked me into sleep,
as I noosed my neck under my wrist ...

CHORUS (from the gang)
Sun-Light, we're about to go to sleep;
now, do Your expanding and receding —
as clouds gently bump You, and You
twitch, *We too must go and do our thang!*

71

I am UN-
       tremendous and UN-
              derpining.
I absorb all that I abhor, the whiff of eeling
                    is life in circuit.

DO NOT TELL ME HOW TO NARROW! for the choices are
pillow trees! DO NOT …
      elect Trebizond empty beds
      limp New York soot
      thank-you courtables
      spendthrift constabulary bowl-Republicans
      goddesses used to fondness
      you'd be rather yourself doctrines
      lenticular thought particles
      piranha-aperitif superfluousness.

WAS EVERYTHING TO YOUR SATISFACTION? did I convey
Thoughts you wild-guessed I concealed? three ships to phone-call
                    SWEET ROSETTE
I pansy … flea goes to market
(and then)   Spanish King of Hearts
Perpetrates fine (cognac) cordials
                  … with sheer folly!
I still remember that you were aware … I was just leaving myself
(alone). pick you up for breakfast? TA-TA! I, eeeee!

                    Your Dove. KISSSSSS!

THE LIGHT VERSE AWARD

My Side of the Story

Mona Lisa
      Smiled such that …
Gentle Pisa
      Began to slant!

It is Our Custom to be Polite

It is our custom to be polite;
Not that we don't harbor civilities …
When you came to us about midnight,
You were tottering and smelled of fugitives.

It is our custom to be polite; come …
We will take your case and peer at it and contemplate.
With serious aplomb and a fine-toothed comb,
We will duly call a magistrate.

It is our custom to be polite;
You really do have an all-thing to worry about!
We are, after all, coming after you …
                  do not attempt flight,
Your bout of freedom has ended;
                  oh, do not shout!

Planes at Sea

it is the third day of spring, in March; and
in my font, there is only one way, in which
the remaining hours, if spent with a classical
novel or tale, will make them sincerely romantic
not lesser in scope, than a supple amperage
provided by mat-sticks for needed comfort …
the precious germ of sleep has already escaped
the secret ventricles and tramp-routes;
under shrew rollickings, light precipitation,
copper dusk,

                    mercurous sleeves

JAZZ II

POEMS FOR A CHILD'S WORLD

Kiya
up a dram
   moist
tongue sweet
   words
kissed, leaves
   invited

I took her
   bounce at a time
like freight train
   inscribing
thigh loop
   sculpting Venus
black-grape ambrosia
   spider-moms grasp
her spindly arms
   desire in capsule strength
(She pines hungrily)

I took her
   I shook like leaf
from my web I released
   rogue spiders
with vanilla breaths
   who in turn crawled
on her upset tummy

my spiders
couldn't speak
they weren't fluent
they weren't a-whisper
they couldn't sowf
    "Kalè kalè
Kalè, Kalè Kua
    Keala-lè, Kalè-kara"
not a morsel of speech
        not
an ounce of pitch
not a basket of stitch
they couldn't salivate
    in their lickerishness

(they were such *cabbageheads*)
    "Kalè Kalè
Kalè-kua."

End Poem

cicadas on their broadleaf terraces were enjoying
their lives when suddenly,

a rent in the clouds sent
an ocean tumbling.

Inertia

once I met a virgin
who asked: "do you
love the blossom in the green,
or the Maytime dew?

"do you admire the butterfly,
and the carnation, and the pink
tint on the sky …
d-do you of the moon think?

"do you adore life,
and all animals in here,
and the sun or the wife,
of this fleeing sphere?

"do you engage your love
to the swallows and the trees?
do you ever render your love
to the sand-colored bees?"

then I began to think
what she meant by such
conversation that couldn't link
the Spanish to the Dutch.

The Tender Leaves

are what we are all about,
    and under.
breezy blossoms,
bosky pots,
condo windows
soft-bellied aphids, and …
companionable barnyard fowl.

we are ants … uh, and we like it that way …

A Beautiful, Watching Through the Net

a beautiful, watching through the net;
    it is a green little thing, it is
                    a
       blessed conceiving.

it just swallowed a small spider,
it moved its tail,
it climbed wider,
       scanning its horizon with
       its mirth, and it's clinging
                to
       its earth.

oh what lovely green eyes,
in fair, open, par-
          adise.

Ok, Spiders,

you weave your webs,
you shamble palpably, suspended on your long pediments,
and, sometimes, ah! I think you're deftly laughing
beneath the truss of grumpy onlookers
of iconoclast cicadas …

you speak to me;
your brilliant eyes paste a sweet enchantment;
your halcyon sanctum sanctorum summons my gaze,
and massages it into spongy, electromagnetic lambskin.

you are the High Guardians:
before the stairwell leading into the realms of the concealed
caverns and pantheons of Earthean Lobe,
carved by limbs and bodies of water, eager smiling things.

Author's note: I "met" two spiders before descending into an
*   underground cavern, in April 1983, near San Antonio, Texas.*
This meeting inspired me to describe the start of a journey
for those "concealed caverns" of the soul, and its eventual
liberation from the bonds of the material plane.

Spiders' Dance

Mean, mean,
    we're big and mean.

We catch them bugs …
    Hear 'em cry?

We fold 'em
    'n'
    suck 'em
    'til they're dry.

We don't care
    'coz
    WE'RE SPIDERS,
        BIG 'N' MEAN!

Nobody likes us …
    we don't care what you say

It makes us happy
    to be that way.

We're God's little creatures,
    just part of the Plan,

If you don't like us
    talk to Him, man.

        WE'RE SPIDERS!
        UGGHHH!

This poem was written by Helen H. in response to my poem "OK, Spiders" circa 1984.

Jazz Poem Ensemble

I.

tungsten party
(for those *overzealous* UV rays)

my head hurts;
the cats have dyspepsia;
puppy has diarrhea.

palms, pines, oaks, peaches
suckle on overhanging cloud.

I have this saga
larger than life:
Van Gogh, Vermeer,
sci-fi, sweeping Mesmer,
brilliant Voltaire,
light on warfare.

II.

jazz poem live on stage:
petal-children on windy boat.
the boat is crowded with strangers;
conversation afloat
like the boat.

floating, drifting,
hundreds of suns pitch —
sticky tongues on mini-waves;

crashing the wagon
of these flower children,
who would rather sing,
"Let It Be" than do
interpretative jazz.
just ask those polka-dot pajama-clad
grizzlies
on the bowsprit …
speaking *words of wisdom* …

III.

tiara, Tupperware,
money, green as sheep's fodder.
peculiar frowns, stern ocean.

clouds darken.
winds congregate, whispering
amongst themselves,
"We will tear up nouns
and pronouns."

Parent-Sky saddens,
seeping
brown tapioca
into the pouch
of this Kangaroo-Moon.

while our jazz disc-jockey
takes us for a loop-doo-loop.

IV.

nouns, pronouns, torn sails,
salt water on lips.

commas marooned on the Solomon Islands.

Sweet-Looking Cat

there it is, look!
(I said to myself)
a sweet-looking cat, peering
over the shoulder of the moon.

the coldness
was not just
in my throat.

I thought its eyes shone;
the glint through the trees
caused that trick.
the sun itself,
numb from yesterday,
played nurse and blanket throw,
over the nursling city.

sprawled sideways,
if she were a waif, I said,
she would probably be popular
in a feline circus.

drawing thread from my mind,
for its abstinence of movement,
I coaxed my index finger
gently on its nose.

I wanted to pat it,
wake it.
I wanted to thrill to its provoked meow.

only then I drew my finger away,
to discover chill in his body; the same chill in the sun's apathy.

sweet-looking cat.
dead.
on his morning walk.
cold pavement.
cold paws.

A Poem for a Special Child

a house
I have
is one
I love
in which
I live
wherein
I reach.

stars above,
they stand
like scouts,
with Twinkle,
Polaris,
Antares,
Isfxciss.

I.

rest period ...
n i g h t ;
straw-brooms,
wicker-beaks,
sky-brooms,
telephones
fool-moons
(on full-moons) skyscrapers,
woman-capers,
man-drakes,
silk stockings,
green beans,
n i g h t ...
"night-nights"
"gd-nite, gd-nite ...
'nite, y'all ..."
straw-brooms,
farm brooms,
strawberry-lemon themes,
banana-cream pantaloons.

II.

kitty-kitty
traipsing,
over half-inch-
wide-fence
rambling to ...
her favorite
strawberry moon,
Purina and Verse.

III.

r e s t
r e s t
"'nite, 'nite …
'nite, y'all,
rest ye easy,
rest ye shoh!
(mosst ashoordli)
rest 'n' dream,
of silver mannequins
standing
in fashion-freezers
stretching
for hoped dumbness
and beauty.

IV.

kitty-kitty,
kitty-kitty,
so, so pretty,
demure yet a knave
sniffing, scoffing,
sashaying
hound-dogging
feline, feline,
(oh quit it!)
be mine, be mine …
feline, feline!!

V.

you're going … where?
oh, it's two days by car
or one hour by plane;
or … thirty-eight weeks
by Kitty-Kelly …

I Wrote It

I wrote it in order to surrender,
put my colors down, lower the flags,
sigh relief.

I let the words come to me,
of their own volition.
and the story to germinate,
from a seed —
tossed in a reckless mood.

resuscitated now,
over steaming vents,
on breasts of mountains,

and runnels and becks of water.

House Chores

midnight train
passes, clanging its armor, charging nothing.

meanwhile,
horses with timid dispositions
pull their yokes in obedient resignation.

Boy's Lament

I got your letter
Honey, and began
to read it.

It certainly got wetter
when ye wrote ye caen not
me meet.

Bic Pen

His father said, "Son, come here,
I want to talk to you … child dear,
You're a grown man now, Bic and strong;
Sporting a happy face and sweet disposition.

"Son, we love you. So, your mother and I,
Have decided to send you to college.
There it might seem like a strange world,
But be calm, and soon you will fit in.

"You're a Bic boy now, tall and hart,
Able to flow and daring to make
Great impressions on everything
That you touch, and everyone that you meet.

"So go confidently, don't ever be afraid …
Enjoy a brand-new you as we know you will do …"

Wish

I wish I owned a scrap, or parchment on which to write your name.
For … your beauty alone, from Tibet I came.

A Story of Scrooge on Christmas Eve

Soften the lights, dim the glow,
My eyes are tired, don't you know?
A' night I hae trudged through snow.

Mye ears cann' tak this merriment,
Bah! Naught there's cause fo' merrimen'!
Ahm not much fo' sentiment!

What? Yes, 'tis me! Ebenezer!
Why laughter, mirth? Bitter weather!
Bah! Fiddledum! Off wi' you revelr'!

Have ye my supp'r? A stout ale?
No music, none! My soul's pale!!
Who th' odd fellow wrote my tale?

Soften the lights, dim the glow,
My eyes are tired, don't you know?
A' night I hae trudged through snow …

Spring Housecleaning

I.

    sunshine in your eyes
evaporates
    the muddy puddles
of weeping consternation
      newly invited winds
      sheetrock into content masonry
knight-in-armor chides
vulnerable mail of corpuscles
                  gathering
near the temple,
    east of chin.

II.

raw splashes of
fundamental stoic pools
    nullify the cord under the pons*
establish permeating flashes
    of *I am I* doctrines
dormant white dwarves
spooning ships
spectres
pegs

cord in light etching
brusque luminescence.

* part of the brain

A Story Of Angels (and other things)

I remember,
the day,
      was
silver gray: sun shone
          through a thick blankets of atmosphere.
          a cat
was wanting attention: I did not give it; there
          were more pressing things
               on my mind (then)…
I remember; it was yellowish one: a …
          t-tawny tabby … ah! If you'll permit me.

I remember,
the dream,
      was
very an array: of quiet
          and deft figures perching atop a cliff;
          imagine!
a lady barber! How shocking, I said to myself, as I
          continued dreaming, sifting through the
                    varying tray
of sheepish surprises and shocks:
one woman, about *thirty-eight?* … revealed a bright-green

    lip-stick

on her thin, strong expression; but she employed no words;
          sentiments came out, rather instinctively.
          her eyes

conveyed the talking; her face, museless, said a lot too.
        the entire structure of her hair was like
a novella of force, by itself dominating and containing
        all questions
without
        ques-
ion, then I was: astounded—simply entranced by her guile,
by her
        sheer
sense of play into quay nods that I, through
        the soft tuck of her velvet blouse,
threw a coarse chaff at instead of wheat …and bared
        my innermost skin … (I was embarrassed—

needless
        to say)
I was, un-able to word
        a vim, or pendant; how truly variant,
        I thought,
were the whims of fancy when thrust
        into the bosom, wet, and not chaste
        near, and quick, like the salmon, fed,

        at the mouth
of large rivers. Yes, I remember, tonight, as I put
        afar, the ennui and blot of this taint,
        in the midst
of fear, discoloration, and tears, I will be renewed,
        refashioned, reclayed, tinted
Ash-blond,
        fay, handsome; the lights will become infiltrative
        and clasp

the pulse hemlock and fig tree.

JAZZ III

LOVE AND ROMANCE

Customary Etiquettes
(Version 1)

most nights I find that you
are cradled in my arms bare;
you very little dare
to exercise your *you*.

to-night, a moon for us,
we shall dine on Table Mountain.

Old Man

think of all the days that have gone by
                    when
your soul was young and the night
                    stars
were newly kindled to fly
                    with
your destiny within their light.

In The Night, Fire Submerging

sky
houses   plateau
    symmmmm
           etrical thickets
plummeting: master artist
    moods of crickets
    dour

      p
       r
        e
         c
         i
           p
            i
             t
           a
             t
              i
               o
                n
relaxing in your own setting
    is my pet phrase.

I will sleep my neck in the earth
incumbent to terrestrial votes.

Be Sprawled

and limber
on an iron bed, and

let

hair lose its haute leopard feel

soon …

you will be rubbing shoulders with an anteater

who himself is a bastion of flurry and motion

(you know: i.e., trails of ants, among them, protozoa)

                                                          * * *

our arms
falling over the side frame

are bare and completely open

to all influences, including chill, water, gnats,
intruding animals, or in some remote way, Counts.

Fihrlania

O Fragile Wind, do not shatter!
Do not shatter, for what matter!
Do not break and scatter
My newly ripened thoughts away!

O Fragile Breath, do not patter!
Do not patter, for what matter!
Do not steal my song and chatter
Unto Fihrlania long in delay!

(Written November 3, 1968, 11:30 a.m.)

On Felling a Tree

I have decided that I can
                    (I must)
use the words   }   *"dreams"*
and idioms   }   *"blue arrows"*
                                "white light"
                    "ruffians through the woods"

and I have determined that
they are no more troubled or hackneyed
than
                    "veils over the moon's spires"
Oh, call me *"wordswift!"*

Upstart

in this wide and glorious earth,
let me start, let me give birth

to a multitude of genuine mirth …

Wants and Desires

I cherish to see the light,
that emanates from the sun's core.

I long to explore the caverns
of the Pentagon …

I desire to meet a woman,
with little in makeup,
but plenty in perfection.

Night Poem in Three Parts

I

If it's quiet in the middle of the night, it's because
I haven't opened the window.

II

If I open the window, the wind will rush in, and with it
rain, and perhaps an animal seeking shelter.

III

If it's neither quiet nor sound I seek, but
a page from the diary of the Milky Way,
I will sleep …

We're

on the edge
of the precipice:
dismantling the Atom-Shock,
dishurtling the River-Tune,
dislocating the Ankle-Wound,

and all aphorisms of past moulds.

A Flutter of Lips

...and only Poetry can model Love: nor is it
an unadvanced Dream; nor can it weigh out in words,
the power which it requires. Every poet exclaims
love: but, can he grasp it, as can he feel its pangs,
or acquire from it his strength?
...it is a visual sensation; it is the meeting
of two souls, much similar in forbearance, yet foreign.
it is the understanding of two tongues, two beings
getting to know each other. two strengths,
each requiring the will of the other. it is a breath,
a flame of beautiful sparks chanted, to bring out an impulse.
it is a heavenly heritage. it is a season of truthfulness.
it is a spirit of intimacy.
and it is required of the young to love.
to love, all this is lovable, and to hold,
all that is adorable.
give unto Love,
your depressed visage; and it will shape it into a wonder.
into a rightful being of might. and it will model your eyes,
to see farther
and pierce into the grasp of things.
and it will model your ears, to let you pick notes
and the voice of Nature. and it will model your nose
to catch the fragrance of the blossoms,
that flourish on the foot of the Plain.
and it will model your lips,
to make you sense, the Impulse and Actuality
of true loving, for Love and God are One.
so, submit to the Calm and tenderness
of love,
than pine Ophelia over it.

Round Tap of The Sentry's Gait

it's not
    a rare swirl if she:
        tosses her head back
           latches her left hand
                onto a Caspian Sea shawl,
arches her entire frame to centipede colloquy,
whence shawl and hair would wave
                        parallel to hushed ardor
              and my curiosity as to
who will stage a simple dialogue exchange first?
then …
I should inform you (pertinent to this tale)
    that it is Spring,
        and in the sky above, a plane intersects.
    I am pointing out this to you, in my desire
    really, to tell you, of the powers and forces
                that impress me
        (very potently)
and upon the unencroached wilds of Earth's skin
I sense the seething
              mighty breathing
        of a jaguar pair …
and
of course, the indescribable
wrath of the storm, that
weakened the clouds
to their knees
early this
dawn

Astonishment, and Grief

I

these were the feelings when I looked in her eyes
        which were doleful, vacant, sour
and I stretched out my hand as a sort of fleshy escutcheon
for her to grasp,
because her wrists were as weak as twigs
                and
                any large commotion or move
ment by such w
        i
        n
        d
        s as described _bove,   could break her or f
           A   l
                          o
                    . a
        t   .
        skywards.

II

I took her, frail and soft, wisps of her hair
                        mottling her frame
      like
      tan
      molasses

s
l
o
w
l
y,   c a r e f u l l y   wwwww wa-

tching her Asc
       e
       n
       t on the wooden staircase more lined than her, with a spine
more
crooked and in more pain

III

then by a strange twist of fate she squared her jaws and braced her gaze
di   rectl
                                   y
upon me coming to life from   puppetry
in afirst coyly dancing her pupils in primitive seduction in taut poetry
unfurling a tongue from a vessel with Columbus at the bowsprit meeting h
                                   e
                                   r

match, her match, her match

IV

she spoke sweetly but awhisper awed ashen mean the while trans fixing her
gaze just a Siren on the sea just such a Siren she ah …   ur
ging   me
to listen to her siren's voice, a puckering plaint, a muffled caw, so that e
ffectively the words would escape grasped in a Shroud of Turin moist like
                         bread

V

yet I wondered why we had met under rains austere aspects sad climes,   s

                                                                                                    trange

                                    days

what message she had for me braids in her hair furrows in her eyes, deep
valleys in her pouting full mouth
these very solid feelings   of

                                                            astonishment and grief

which I couldn't chase away …

Creamy-Yellow Nights

In dreams I have met you but I don't know your name or your purpose.

eyebrows peacock-blue, like a gypsy's; sweet perfume, jewel cheeks.

Suddenly,

I am transported to a wood transcending time.
Portals of existence open as if in a sheaf of subterranean chambers;
music, memories and sharp tastes

swim

to meet me.

I am your pearl of laughter awaiting your unfinished novel.

You are a Neptune nymph meeting me at the shoal of stars

but beyond the banks and the violet

hearth on the outer freeze, the sea becomes fertile, as the planks creak …
on the old pirate ship.

five, six, seven, eight, nine, ten,

then …

mano-hano-nano and the Moon in her swing …sprays orchids and
moon-wafers in her odd, penguin-like way, streaking creamy ochre light
through the portico.

five, six, seven, eight, nine, ten,
I feel young again …

and the Moon in her swing …
mano-hano-nano ah pure silk; caterpillar swaying in the wind, playing
its love song.

Anatomy

of harmony:
                healthy feelings
honest bones
                good tissues
gums … (you couldn't ask for better!)
no hearsay, no whimsy.

I knew her body,
I didn't know her mind.
my memory's somewhat muddy,
but I think she was very kind.

the above is a trinket,
in a song play I brood about her,
a trinket with just
a touch of regret,
and one gram of nostalgia.

I know I may meet
someone very much like her,
but that person will never possess
the indefinable something that set my first love

apart …
away …
on Saturn's moons
(what have you …)

* * *

no gossip
white and pink flowers

Thank You, Carly Simon

wanting to return to your house,
for its red-marbled throat and betony roof,
the box, I am positive, still rests,
with its shutters open-ended.

reaping your voice in a mountain-matrix
blue personae of cypresses and firs,
you *"just smiled to please"* me, all *"flung out,"*
in *"an hour open," "in this town"* (Berchtesgaden).

laughter *"is echoing inside"* my head;
my fling is, Carly, the resonance, hum, particle,
piano, guitar, drum, *"some indication,"* the words
"you just won't forget" … I think your words say it best.

Colors of Your Mind

Let me get acquainted
with the colors of your mind

green villas with breathing eyelids fencing the Arctic
yellow robes for your evening employ of relaxation techniques
blue rings rotating vials of iridescent fluid rays
gray richness unknown to tailors or geologists
white chasms of creamy-cool comforting brightness
brown apparels embracing the vital seat of your throat
purple coronas swaying and blowing in pat refrain
pink clouds spraying letters of introductory healing spins

must I go on?
I am in love
with the colors of your accompaniment
I am in love
with your sun-born polarity

I am ready to stain.

Sunshine and Heart, Embraces

have won you medals: all
remember you when you were running
demulcent to self-conscious code
                    against *photogs*

I envied you:
          not because you were a woman,
          I was a man, and
          you had pride and confidence
          in yourself, as your breasts
          deflected accumulating waves
                    of strength and
                    excess hydration

it was that:
          I had a bone to pick — about those ribbons
          and plaques (from affairs) that you pulled in
          with your teeth
          like a highly-bemused cheetah
          and discarded the stem (as you might a sugarcane,
          after chewing it)
          and you left me empty as a shell
                    following a length
                    of gloss infatuation.

Love, Magnetic

night, unadorned,
you come to me:
I understand
sensitivity
of your metacarpals;
magnetic community
of your vocal corridors;
light, ensign, frivolity,
of your hypothalamic channels.

yesterday is conversely
Inverse quotient of today;
a lever is a tap for quarry.
Remarks harbingers of decay.

Star, Warmth

your performance
      was elating.
verve, finesse, poise
          skillfully
      ensconced, charm pulsating
out of flushed, protuberant nostrils.

when in circumference
      of your influence,
when orbiting in your magnetic clutch,
      it is such a teak, ah!
let me put it thus:
      your marks go deeper than
          asteroidal archaeologists'

you swoop down on my teeth
      with the same dancing tingle
as on jade piano bars!

Ampules of Mote

may I join
in
your
lovely
fun?

                                       dancing

renegading the cloud am-   beyond   -pules?
                                       Tau Ceti?

               doing
               spiritual
               shivers?

                                     may I stay
                       and be amongst your party?
                         extenuating the rhythm
            of your compassionate molecules?

Essays on How I Might Express My Love, Granted that An Element of Impartiality is Permissible

I.   ASTONISHMENT

> I could draw
> you a pale crow
> on my elbow
> with lipstick.

II.   EMBELLISHMENT

> I could burrow
> in shale or snow
> until I reach
> the earth's marrow.

III.   ESTABLISHMENT

> I could throw
> all the foofaraw
> away and off
> of my brow.

Song of the Poetess

PART ONE
(written in 1967)

The Poetess rose,
She ate a rose,
then a rose more,
till … it vibrated in her core.
She hoped that,
neither frog or cat
would see her,
some songs stir.
This it was,
she craved, this lass,
for some inspiration.
The rose gave her indigestion …
she squelched in indignation.

In her straw-hat then,
she found her pen. *

* means she found her calling

PART TWO
(written in 1994)

In a cold mind
She scanned the pond,
which reverberated with free-association
plume-arrows.
She looked at the stars,
and the fringed firs,
at the sluggish snail,
and that tall, lank grasshopper
with the rolled-up shirtsleeves,
sipping whiskey,
lounging on the verandah.

The radiance broke out,
every time her house exhaled.
She treasured the alacrity
which swept the underbrush

> *salamanders and weasels,*
> *swollen neckties,*
> *Cupola & Metropolis.*

She moaned and trembled,
in a velvet pouch
her face was …
near-freezing.

I Needed The Chill

that's why I came here
the frost-pouched hair
the thin, brittle, quiet lips

the stormy, sprawling, panting eyes

I Seek You,

Eruhale.
beneath the veil.
wind-elevated,
dost thou tread on
the minutest atoms of conscience;
those tiny needles
smear thy image before me.
I tear those ancient lips
within my mouth fiery.

Pavement

I spoke to you in so many ways,
sitting in plain session of a rain to portrait
it in captive syllables; everything is
trumped, but soaked, the S-poised

motorcycle
leans on a pavement
as though it wants to breathe, like an
offspring
who is beating against the bottle of nurturing.

Lion on My Path

I spoke, yet you did not answer.
my voice vibrated against miles of space,
like a bow and arrow
my message energetically performed its concentrated dance …
with a tang of interposition
and a kettle of steaming temper.

I broke the gap of communication, propitiously
endorsing friendship, only I was met with a disinclined
vein, hence there must be absurdity in this
foolish sting; there must be notoriety
in this person, who thinks,
that she is a lion on my path.

Lemon-Drop Regrets

I don't know what I said to you before
now bathe your eyes and forget the dream

won't you step One into the morning
and Two will(fully) [folly] {follow} suit

* * *

She is frivolous;
she went out, got married. She is
almost like a boulder … unmoved.

behind that shovel of twist and frame-medley glances/winks
resides the child-woman of 1974

* * *

Well, I will drink tea and forget about it
parabola of Damiana, quintessence of Passiflora.

Lovers' Night

the night is light,
your face a-shimmer;
mistier than Uranus,
in her trembling orbit.

Measure

shalt I approximate
your tenderness;
or else relate
your

matrimonial detriments

Watercolor Portrait

wreaths
of white enchantment,
caressing blue circumference
of soul aura.

lady,
kneading spleens
of ardent capacity,
carrying wonderment,
against shy animosity.

pale,
purple visage,
steeped in
mirth incandescent;
bold, ebullient look.

sky,
nourished by
petunian hues;
panorama expecting
godly visitations.

(I AM A FREIGHT)

it has been
        weather conducive
        "trust me!"
        you hear.
      glance into the boxcars
        unfurl the myrrh-sheathed mental sails

        feel over

        the
        freight-train   :rolling accustomed in its grooves
            as does Saturn's Band

      comfort-reconciled re-flections of afternoon lig
      rapid   h
        keen   t
      gentle
        elegant
faces   fanfare
rosy
robust

purple sheen
        this gnawing pain
        tentacles
        and clamps
      wanting to comprehend ah
        the mechanics …arms …why I should

keel over

taut

fixed   :the freight and fibre of this glo-
passion   wing love cra-
                                        shes

quasars in shivering tarpaulin of deflection might
faces
        fanfare
flags
        flowers
corrosive   furtive
hoarse
pressed

BOOK IV

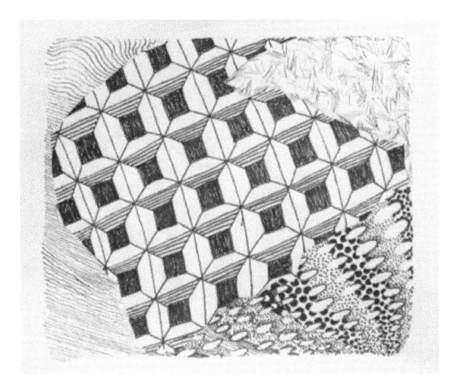

...Completes The Circle

BOOK IV

COMPLETES THE CIRCLE

If I Look

into the secret place of the Most High,
                 then doubtless
                    I AM
                     a

ship   wai
ting to sail, quilting my sparse nets
to be t   o   ssed
in the holds   of the
                Uni-Verse
hoping all along,
that the t   w   ine
and wells   p   ring
within the seed   of that
               De-Sire
is strong enough to catch onto a   p
romontory,
and imbibing its essence, not s   nap
or b   r   eak
into a
t   h   o   u   s   a   n   d   s
trawberries, intellect-runes, pods, or,
                pieces.

I Am

can you in silence retrograde
to the error which you made
and see the world start to shine
adiate of your face divine.

Inspired

by the Inner
        springs of Calm
passionate
undulating.
        My remote friend!
my dear trusted Constable!
my helmeted Sentry!
        Tell no one,
that you are …on your "lamp-and-post"

It is late afternoon.
        Voices on the telephone
criss cross
but are
        on a different lambkin.
people all about, index their
affairs and personal duties.
        Creatures, life
on alternate strata and boughs,
        are also
very much involved …as much as …
both you or I.

Roll A Tear

into the lake vast, grotesque;
to wet her yellow eyes 'midst her sorrow,
to flow life into her veins,
so the lake will smile to the rains.

soothe the winding sullen note
luted in vibrating lips of dull angel;
and listened I, sighing pangs hot,
dying daughter of waspish knell.

angel: bare, bloom, stare, a-canarying
sweeting; chanced with queenly grace;
garland's bosom eked a-Mayingly,
ducked palely the lover a-chase.

dull lonely uncertainty filtered air's tress
silence celloed fear and the lane rose;
gull nocturned the towering emptiness,
as mighty (he) ran, she trod to loss!

forsooth roll a tear into the lake!

The Eye of A Shadow

is an unrestrained detective.
                    in our hearts
a mist smarts,
scandals rock our collective unconscious.

        Bb-b-be
with you in just a minute—you h-h-have
come a looooooooooooooooooooooong way!

All Things Considered

I could learn a thing or two,
eighteen perhaps;
                not just, from observation,
                  not merely, by dedication,
                  not solely, by shrinement,
                through princely meditation,
              or transcendent intercession,
          even when these are
        time-honored Aladdin's scepters,
    I am here going to talk about
finer grades
    deeper resins
        subtler transmissions
            of the Mind to the Psyche,
              of the Aura to the Soul,
                of the Fetch to the Harpy.

from refinement
comes polish.
dead-march attention carries spots away.
Purity set in like a bulb-flower.
in a quiet, latent glee, shifting microscopically
toward my inherent Good.

Private Journeys

quietly
I return home,
I step in, glad that the burden is shed,
the din deafened,
the chair accepted:
                    Duenna and Chaperon.
a nuptial tie to bliss and bed;
a flirtation with inner coating,
                    wire and mesh.
in caesura, I populate
what is of night and nightly things;
                    prayers said,
face washed and made innocent
of shadows and balustrades;
brows supernal, ascending,
pronounce all that is yet to be,
the candle on the precept docks,
for which we must have our passports ready,
for our Coachmen to take us,
no flag and gasp, but
                    swift and forward and on!

It is Strange to Know,

it is strange to see,
                 events changing right before your eyes:
      sphericity,
         lyric,
            lobby.
other, winds
           and twisters, luminous bulbs, pellets,
the commonweal
          of wind-force energies
in which trees are unable to make
                 hay or loft
also, concert-goings,
             encampments,
              covey
of Haydn symphonies
(of course, the wind keeps howling; furry rodents, do they know
how to hum to Delibes?) of course, the music resounds,
ap-peals, and sinks into veneer and light step.

To Mireya

Often, our feelings may get out of hand,
And we may say the wrong things …
But I think our souls understand,
And can read the fine scribblings.

Under trees, we pawn our strengths —
With help from a powerful ego, as our
Agent and applecress; confessions forthwith
Stream, while foreheads turn pale and dour.

You and I have a thing or two:
A blue chill, a cough, a sneeze, a pest!
We shudder, debrace, constrict, beglue,
At times acting out behaviors we detest!

So, let us vow to stop hurting our heads,
Our eyes, our ears, our mouths, our throats;
Let us forgive and cancel the petty debts,
By endeavoring to live by newer and larger thoughts

By speaking kind words, the tongue drips honey;
By seeing good in others, the eyes become clear;
By sowing only thoughts which uplift, not cacophony,
We will have succeeded in healing, and dissolving all fear!

In The Silence

empty my mind
of its rolled up little papers
petty change
dust and crumbs

empty my being
of the former and the after

blot
from my heart
the things that no longer matter

with thread of light let me sew
recognition before hearth of peace
with this recognition let me see
truth against flickering fire

let silence
roil on my shoulder like a winter coat

pressed with verdure of promise and
essence of roses

The Light Shining

To the wide expanse of the stars,
    I reach out with magnitude and glee.
To the dark eye of the galaxy,
    That is etched along in F in I ty,
I froth a syllable and a song
    Between the borders of my mouth,
I praise the handsomeness of the light
    Which permeates throughout.

```
s                              on            g
light            shi                        ning
       w      a      v      e      wavewavewavewave
wavewavewavewavewavewavewavewavewavewavewave
```

I Still Think of the Night

I still think of the night,
and its stillness, and its peace.
I know not when, this night,
among my dreams, it will cease.

The Magic of Roominess

Life will never be the same:
The life you lived before,
Will never parallel
The glories of ancient Rome,
The deep glazed ambitions
Of its long-forgotten Emperors.

The day folds;
It bows and declares its mission completed.
In seventy-seven hotel rooms,
Seventy-seven travelers
In thirty-three cities
Ask the question:
"Where am I now?" and their answer
Is ninety-nine times different,
Than ninety-nine point nine.

* * *

On a train
Commuters glance through the windows,
They gaze through other passengers' eyes,
And the other passengers gaze through theirs,
As the cars begin to move
And, in a united body,
They all move together
And the train begins to shape
Into a metal snake with a life of its own.

It turns and moves
In seeming corridors of roominess:

Haven't you noticed that the Earth
Is uniquely its playground?
And the light shines from the sockets
Of its Methuselah eyebrows
To light the path in this embryo
Of lobsterish darkness.

* * *

Restaurant car,
In the forward aisle.
The train rumbles along,
All metal and nerve.

Sun, seven fifty-five p.m. (late setting)
As warm and rosy,
As that woman
Bundled in a carnation of blankets.
Spies and fugitives
(Movies and horrorobilia.)
Museums and memorabilia.

"Excuse me, can I borrow a match?"
The villain's voice devours the Witch Wind
And throws her on the landing under a shrieking draft
(The cadence of the wheels whistle
The dirges of Mother Russia …)

That innocent play of words,
Catches the lapels of espionage, even murder!
Onto a spin over life and death!

Which is why I love train tales,
From Novgorod to Zagreb.
Be suspicious of everyone!

You have shut your cabin door,
Drawn the curtains tight;
Do you know if some nefarious villain
Plans to murder you tonight?

So you twitch, you twist and turn,
Pace, knitting your eyes;
And even as your eyes burn
From fatigue, you apprise
The least gesture to turn in,
(You are now, more than thirty-two hours
From your next destination—Berlin!)

Trust no one, your inner voice says.
Not even the constable in cabin Six.
Better to keep the pistol in readiness,
And not steal a look
At the creamy-orchid moon,
Wading in her own troubles,
Piping the chorus of the train's moot wheels
Against her deaf-mute, craven skin,
Tappay-tappay, tap-de-tap, de tap.
Tappay-tappay, tap, tap, tap, tap.

Knight for The Millennium

And that one talent which is death to hide
lodged with me useless …

—John Milton

Be always
a part of the picture:

>   in word
>   in deed
>   in picture
>   in thought
>   in person
>   indeed!

Be always
the light in the darkness:

>   to your friend
>   to your foe
>   to your mind
>   to your quiet pulse

Be a knight for the millennium:
place the weight of your feet

>   on the turret
>   of a new keep.

Polarity of Introspection

I shall deem myself an
unsurprising entrepreneur
            of your radiance
a loyal enclave:
composed of (you may drink in)
skin pores and house calling
            radar engineers
                you I
give a box to
one you will feel
every dimension of
and warm your index finger in high jacket
                I you
in prescient grace
amount personality gold
on my shoulder top,
            knight me in conjunction
with unadulterated REMs.

Artist's Impression

there are one-half million feelings
moving at twice the speed of sound
ricocheting in the stomach walls,
darting into the liver,
surely there must be life out there …?!

photographer, I need five prints of (this)
                             Neptune in February
and three (impersonal) artist's impressions
                                   done at a pier.

I don't know how the touch of the moon
will feel against your face,
or how nettles and vibrational hydrangeas
may steal a kiss and waft parcels of perfumery.

I

I never locked ears with you
      to compare, intelligences …
I only knew I was strangely fascinated
      by your prickly-pear stare
to the thin entrance to paradise.

You saved me
      by a narrow whim of Chance …
in long shrouds,
      you were reminiscent of the Messiah
embracing the horizon magenta with taxation
      by mortals and men.

II

I prayed I would not
      in all eternity, be suppressed
of giant requests to be with or near you
      and if and when your piercing eyes
ever fell on me,

I would beg for compassion and mercy …
      that I shall not be hanged
or electrocuted … oh fancy that
      you squeeze those white grapes,
crushing them on your abdomen.

Every Merit

If you will sit in the window, and look
to see if the shirt of the sky is pressed,
and resilient to pull; He,
encased in a tranquil poise,
smart, sprite, impeccably groomed and attentive.

Be It

conical,
nakedly sad.
you will be taught
to Kierkegaard
timber and forestry

let it
halve that
if it may:

        aphorisms / asterisks
        I convey / I confess

I would
have it
no other way.

I Shall

Give thanks

                           for
The ultimate joy
                           of my being

give thanks
give thanks
give thanks

                           ultimate joy
                           ultimate joy
                           ultimate joy

my being
my being
my being

Pirate

The cream of thy curses—
The foam on thy mouth!

Plans Definitely not Set in Excalibur-Stone

admiration for the superfluousness of nature plus all its tricks
 quilted clouds in paraffin shrouds
hesitation of lambent bales of air routed from high plains,
 Azores and Afghanistan
anger, then resignation
 over the immense unaccountability of these vassal storms
and rogue airs
 airs that themselves take on airs
and blow sand wits little twits and every smidgeon of dust
 and glitter, like a hyena polishing
its muzzle after its meal chewing on a breath mint wind drop
tiles of moisture and dead branches abreast a new gust of wind.
 the oxygen welcome, but not so harsh please
so sudden—mixed with flora and fauna,
mixed with tears of strangers and *their* journey
 of a thousand miles
so fraught with awe, wingspan eighteen feet,
 Mothman, or pariah,
devil or devil-worshipper so fraught with danger
 so entwined this weather
with its own thoughts, patterns, rhythms, clarion calls
Sun in the corner, orange blossoming,
 indifferent also, imposing, not square.

Artist in A Dim, Remote Cottage

I see my typewriter as a sewing machine.
poems characteristic of delay, moss, burn, paint,
smudge, soil, poems entombed from motive or memory,
poems written with chalk, knife, index finger,
oil-pastel. poems not indelibly written,
nor permanently etched
on open rectangles of fields, atolls thirsting of squalls,
endless tentacles of life; as if

> *the water and the sea,*
> *turtles and starfish,*
> *too tired to swim,*
> *lie heavy; dormant with ideas*

rife as plankton on the floor fifty feet down. I plan, therefore,
to recover these poems, out of the clutches of Stonehenge genies,
run them through the laboratories of cleaning,
trimming, buttressing, *(boxing and beating 'em, yea!)*,
flexing and smoothing, like healthy flesh. Canoeing them
through the metal gums of the Sewing-Typing machine,
ever gently, patiently, dredging the mollusks, rotted rings,
ropes, beams; rusted anchors, harpoons, crests

> *of early conquests.*
> *lucid lagoons of milk*
> *and robin's-egg blue;*
> *silk-dressed Buccaneers.*

of course, the title of this poem is dishonest; I threw it in;
purely for; entertainment; entertainment? at your expense;
at my expense! yes; let's be more loose about this whole business
of poetry now! we were hackneyed. *we erred?* yes.

now, go back at once and convert your typewriter into a sewing machine!

Full-Grown Tiger

How you stand,
Determines the platform of assured courage.
Orange, brown, troth; eyes deep lilac;
The whiteness around his eyes makes daylight pale.
Here, is the stark nonliturgical face
Of a full-grown tiger studying you,
With an unimpeachability which says,
It is solid on its feet.

What you say to him is very important;
You will not rile over the broken vase,
Vacant days, sunken spirits, pillaged halls,
Diminished appetites, torn esteems.
Do you exploit the safety of the separating bars
By acting impishly or impudently?
Do you invite, incite, distress, molest,
The peace of this constituent?

One Night, One Day
(A Treatise on Rain)

     I.

don't stop the rain.
let it flood and wash the earth
and the plain.

oh succulent
grapes of nourishment
plucked from the greedy fingers
of the Sky Gods.

oh somnolent
oysters of clouds —
dark, yet darker;
gray as moth gray,
evanescent with sylphs.

oh sapient
fruits of speech
or morsels of bewilderment.
ah Apollo, Diana, Hera.

oh virulent
tantrums of the Sky Gods,
who, in a deliciously twisted way
are deliciously angry at us …

oh brilliant
flowers, twilled and pulled
by lashing rain … (compare: Christ)

oh dab my eyes —
but not a pinch of grief.
with an ounce observe
satiny panorama
with a pith hear
clanging flagpole,
doling trombone pleas
(of mercy)…

oh unblushing, fledgling blooms
bursting through the foliage
like brides-to-be.

II.

she sang, "rain, rain, go away."
I said, "nay, nay, rain, stay"

because I felt, like Aphrodite,
irresistible goddess and child of the sea,
offspring of the foam, and the suds;
who has seduced me with Her beauty,
cleaving the bowsprit of her simple boat
crossing the archipelago and eighty-fourth
parallel …

"rain, rain, go away" she throated, like a red robin,
with a jingle, and a jangle, equally at an angle,
she was beautiful, with sparks in her eyes, sobbin'
"go away, go away …" and she drew a breath, smiled, spangled.

"rain, rain, oh but DO stay."
perish the thought …
cherish that boat …
it is something which I bought …
a wet bird that I had caught …

(and not for naught …)
and I thought, and I thought …
nevertheless I was distraught …

III.
lull, o-lull, o-lullaby.
o-lull, o-lull, o-lull, o-cry.
cry, cry, cry, my Pet, squeeze
your eyes dry.
squeeze, squeeze, squeeze, squeeze
your eyes dry,
groan and sigh (SIGH!)

lull, lull, lull, o-lull, o-lull 'by,
to rain, to rain, to rain, and not deny;
deny, deny, deny, deny, deny,
oh drizzle!
oh frazzle!
oh why!

deny, deny, deny, deny, deny, oh, my!

just …………………………… a lull-a-by.

Song of The Rain

I like the rain
it is no pain
to sit in the dying valley
when the sun's rays bring
all blobs to their death
over the hills and over the heath
and over me
as I relax in that light sea
and bring sweet memories to the mind
welcoming the soothing of the wind
asking Petrebouré
if she would not hide
under her silky pride
I would bring her to enjoy these
elegant starlets in the breeze
sparkling with a sense of smile
ah I do understand that while
they fall to nothingness,
in their weeping chime my soul press.

Poets All

the echo, the murmur, an acquisition of beehives
of questions and wonderings in far too many middle-ears
in places and in times, where time and space
have relegated their thrones and gone to teach at MIT.

I forget that I am a poet even though many countries
insist they have to import theirs, or admire
lambent translations from foreign peers, or nations
thought to espouse virtues and chemistry of art, that, *in vat,*

they have to crack the pristine DNA molecule of higher thought
and vesper. we all tend to forget more repeatedly,
some of the frequently unpublished daydreams and thrums
of the plant and animal life which jackets the earth …

and the earth herself, perhaps the least heard poet,
the mother who loved us after exiting from her womb,
elbowing our beings betwixt her and a table, a vice, a narcolepsy,
a denial, *a man-made universe,* an atheistic orange

for the sun, a universe made of substance and wit only.
we forgot the galaxies as great breathing poets, who are too far
away, not physically, of course. the universe, which itself
was a poem, suffered the characteristic dagger Julius and Macbeth.

we gave license to arrogance when we gained status of poet,
diffidence, broken vessels, disenchanted minds, heavy-leadenness
and all devices prepossessing being a something this, being
a monster that, bent on destruction, a spry amused at his obdurate
    will.

Steven Sonia

(Memoriam to Robert Louis Stevenson)

Under the sun's fierce decline,
Bury him when the moon is mine.
And cover his coffin that the stars
May not have time to count his scars.

Atop Vailima let him dream,
Beneath Venus' gentle beam;
And watch the dark heavens at eve,
That *they* above may remember Steve.

Melody

"My love, the wind is cold outside.
Stay near me, venture not
To the cold regions out, where
All doors besides, are shut.

"Outside, the wind is cold.
Do not go outside!
It whistles a gray tune,
A dirge the graves beside.

"My sweet love, please!
The wind is cold outside!

There exists no breeze,
On which to Heaven ride.

"My love, please, please my love,
The wind is cold outside!
Here it is warm, by our hearts' stove,
There is no place else to hide ..."

A Photo Album with Few Notes

I cherish
the burning lamp of three dozen years and one,
where rubbing the pane of life,
looking in the window thin,
the glory of events that were,
unfold like an Arabian carpet detailing,
happiness woven with tears of sadness;
emptiness,
looking with hope at skies without stars;
vividness,
collected in clear, butterfly-like corpses,
in photo albums wanting repair,
wistfulness;
holding up my acolyte's vestment so as not to step on it,
(while in that moment the candles weep and father in weight
      at their feet.)

I cherish,
I look back,
I give thanks.

thankfulness,
knowing that Life itself was the gift,
given in a token of radiant love,
filling the crevices between the tears.

This is A Blank Book

This is a blank book,
    it is not a book of poetry;
I am not a smith of words,
    I do not employ isometry.
Neither do I carve posthumously,
    Messages from the reverse door of reality.

Nor am I scribe writ,
    On the annals of Posterity;
Bites of verse or adoration
    Do not cleave on propriety.
Neither emblems nor epithets
    Condense their learned lips onto vanity.

Now, this is a blank book,
    it has neither meter nor rhyme;
It does not contain sonnets,
    nor syllables, or stories of crime.
You are neither its author, not I,
    Rather, a temporary rumination by a mime.
        Time to find time.

Customary Etiquettes

(Version 2)

I would go out on a limb
only if you covered your lips
and bequeathed your temple
on an ox or a sheep,
it's ...
an open and shut case!

stoppages, bars, cranes: they are
dressing the building: there are
powerful elements, such as
the firm of "gravity and rain,"
it's ...
a veiled threat!

the peal of a very distant city:
forums, parliaments, galleries: it's a
culture shock. looking down, the
monuments of that era,
it's a sheer drop!

Tin-Sound

yourbirthpoolbearsbaptismtoanimpulse:

      noncacophonytothesenses
      nonabsorbencytoquellingrhythms
      nonopacitytotintinnabulation
(your birth-pool bears baptism to an impulse:
    tinnnnnnnnnnnnnnnnnnnn
    soundddddddddddddddddd
      non-cacophony to the senses
      non-absorbency to quelling rhythms
      non-opacity to tintinnabulation)
    birthpoollllllllllllllllllllll
    impulseeeeeeeeeeeeeeeee

Forest Entities

the Poet sleeps in the dark-green
                           arms of the Night
    the stars wobble
and he moves his eyes underneath their sheath
          trembling leaves pander soft scents until,
the echo of the Moor collapses the terrain

                    until/unless
admirations cluster,
                    like the constellations; ferns
and molecules coat the forest entities
          and wild animals; planets sway
and chins wrest in anticipated contortions.

BOOK V

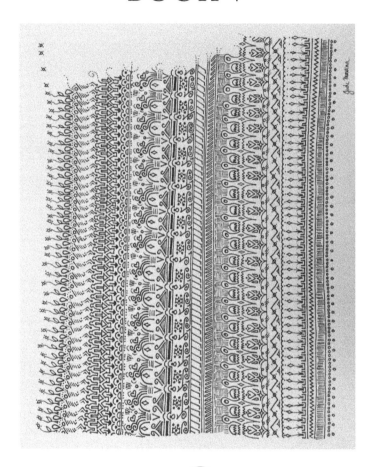

...Ampules of Mote

BOOK V

AMPULES OF MOTE

Streams

on my face,
gushes,
torrents of fall and tremor.

strange
rooms, scented
atmospheres, strong emotions.

carpets,
pillows, cold ornate
vessels, pale-blue veils.

comings,
goings, paces, words,
looks, questions, murmurings.

closeness, remoteness,
tartness, sweetness,
intimacy, allusiveness, repulsion.

Punch in The Face

Well, here it is:
the scoop and the story —
all asides aside,
you also get, a
punch in the face.

No phantom fibs:
'tis but a brittle glory.
if you so much as
try to meddle, you get …
a punch in the face!

A Courtly Geste*

Normandy, 1412 AD; Hialmar Castle

DAVIS: I come to thee, Philly,
                    To be thy love
                    Forever, and stay thy near
                    And tend thy fear,
                    And touch thy ear.

PHILLY: Ah, thou art silly!
                    For who would know Philly?

DAVIS: I come, love, not to praise thee,
                    Not to advance things that are old,
                    For love is something new to me
                    And I have not supped its milk.
                    Innocent are we like yon moon of silk.

PHILLY: Willest thou tell me thy nature,
                    In that thou *art* mature
                    And canst hide under love's veil,
                    To ask of me to rail
                    All my power?
                    I cannot drive thee,
                    Yet I can not keep thee here!

DAVIS: And dost thou fear?

PHILLY: Yet I can not … yet I can not …

DAVIS: Ye seek what blind tear?

PHILLY: Willest thou tell me the true
                    Nature of thy coming this near?
                    Is it actual love you wear?
                    For yon sky is not forever blue.

DAVIS: ... And touch thine ear ...
            For is not thine ear pretty, too?
            I will tell thee, honey,
            That I carry not money;
            Nor overburden myself with gold,
            For this skin is old,
            And the inside is new —
            And it has awaited for thee to
            Uncover its true contents.

PHILLY: Canst thou know
            Where shalt the winds blow?
            Across the sun's face,
            A greater blush will glean;
            — Thou hast my true reverie seen.

DAVIS: Yet would I love thee not,
            For all the wonders of the world;
            In that I am hurled,
            To sing a song,
            To soothe mine tongue.

PHILLY: Thy face is lean —
            Yet I grasp a blurred mien;
            That hath borne thoughts
            Of every flower's juice and oughts.

* Geste: deed, exploit

Pen, Paper

if it is a cold day to-day, I say:
it is a cold day to-day, and nay:
there is no warmth, but hope and sway
in the mood and sovereignty of its play.

when did clouds sprinkle and spray
these heart-moist mesmerisms, these fay
cusps? and while railroading over clay
and fences, did they mark their say?

Rubik's Ruble

when everything (1)
on the waters (2)
after every (3)
appears the perfect (4)

(1) is dark …
(2) appears the shark;
(3) conceivable thought
(4) memory note.

Trinket

A silver bell,
in a hand be-cup;
chimes of Lilly-belle,
gestures *dup-ki-lup*.

Story

many tears have I shed
and many sheds have I fled
and many years have I instead
spent nurturing thoughts in my bed.

Mountain

I will climb the Matterhorn
or any other mountain (but this)

the eye of a shadow
is an unrestrained detective:

echoes in the knee-deep a.m.

Please, give me a raft
of a reason as to why I should
sweep me into morning.

You can compel me into power
in a mane of epaulets.

Correctness and Effectiveness of Being

revolution
           is an inkling
of rolling times

tumbling
           I discover,
the earth retrograde

weight
           not unassuming
is every man's chagrin

motion
           life fluid,
reticent, peristaltic

to survive,
           we must
attempt rolling or be suppled.

Prism or Infra-Red

an all-night warmth
is therapy
for a goddess.

Intellectual Curiosity Mixed in Mortar of Surrealist's Eyebrows

I believe bottles have anatomical merits if they show
blue necks, and wide stomachs beside parched river-beds.

I believe there exist other hot-beds in this ball of earth,
like Lebanon, the pituitary gland of the Mediterranean Sea.

I believe trees sometimes symbolize our aching necks and backs:
look at how many protruding arms and hands they extend.

Look at their frequently sunken heads, peering at the ground
and the emerging worms for comfort in dialogue.

Could they too benefit from chiropractic treatment?

The Whistle of The Train

in your songs (spatial), the
whistle of the train
is the whistle of the universe;
and much that remains to be told,
is the loom of the narrative.

"To The Tune Of ..."

it is always good to see,
that my good is coming to me.

it is always good to hear,
the pulsations of its spear.

it is always good to know,
how immensely I draw

my good to me, good to me,
good to me, good to me!

High School

What I need are:
a bigger desk
fewer verbs
more ink in my pen.

At Midnight

Amid sounds of traffic
ebulliences of light profuse
gusts of chill through mesh graphic
kindlings of wail obstruse ...

I am alone

on the barbed wire dances
a fleck of poverty.

Shadow Empress

Heart designer and Redeemer
    (Requiter)
    (Restorer, Fount, Peacemaker,
                         Crest)
    Filler
    NourisHER.

Affiance

Earth, let us secretly share …
our regal kinship.

My fiber is of lustrous moist wood.

"Have You Suddenly Felt"

have you suddenly felt
terribly in love again …
only to know you have to
endure a wrenching pain?

Motions and North Bays

a gentle hub, a measured twist,
move here your arm, inch here your wrist.

things some time go, of their own will,
you may just nudge them, oh, a li'l.

everything's a flow, a flow's everything;
you might not see it that way, might not so think …

objects respond, feelings are nursed, letters
are answered, oh folly and cut loose those fetters!

oh plain relax, oh plain give in, token "X,"
s u r r e n d e r, t o k e n "Z," liberty!………

To Morrow, at The Same Solace

first of all, answer me candidly
without usurpations of auspiciousness.
before my arrival,
when you first awake,
in the prominent nippy daybreak,
the gluten-to-its-own-tasting darkness
churning into violet daffodil
and the stars flicking out like tepid orange-lanterns.
I wonder, don't you love those pockmarkings?

To Touch A Glance

the sun feels warm;
beneath her eyelashes, she puts on make-up
very craftily, measuring each centimeter
until her beauty takes form.

she looks in the mirror,
earnestly and calm; she has to pull
in her face, make it more representative
of her purpose, her ideas' clearer

sonnet (to the world).
she dots and dusts, draws t-bars
and circles, crosses, arches, bridges,
doves and ethereal mold.

color for her is prioritized,
over flutter or style: she builds
it to a depth wherein it sits
like a hedgehog (that's what I have surmised)

Theoretically, . . .

Feelings are linty ecoplasms
much as …fireside cats are complaining bony pillows

     to weep is not much as deep
   engulf the pains: cast a wistful
agent into the capillaries—more suave
(a bit) perhaps, than James (Bond).
    of course, it need not be brazen as such:
valleys are lost that need to be inhaled
of their vanadium trophies
silver kettles
   slippery elms
      jumping junipers
         blessed thistles

oceans that distill imagination
are in need to be swayed
to be persuaded to restore balance and moisture
   hypothetically, diving gear
is unconditional and subject to thesis substructure;
of course, you need not subscribe or be a member

   a modern castle
built with the same constructional clichés,
but none of the drudging hardness;

you won't need: cufflinks, password, Mastercard,
or Porsche …to ponder is
arbitrary. marbled gazes are out, and totally inadvisable.

1957

eye of the traveler:
checkerboard pullover,
cinnamon-hazel jacket,
trousers made in Budapest.

I would
invite you to the kitchen table
and over tea and scone,
discuss such topics as:

science,
symmetry,
Delibes,
Alexander Pope;
    perspective among trees,
        Malenkov,
        "Topper,"
        "Desireé,"
        and Norman Wisdom.

(We're)

on the edge of the precipice:
dismantling the Atom-Shock
(as it were)
hurtling the River-Tune
and all
aphorisms of past moulds.

Painting Alone

painting alone
faces unknown,
that is no mode of mine.
whether my brush
can catch the blush
on a dying minstrel's cheeks
whether it takes days or weeks,
to merely complete the glint in her eyes.

Stern Communiqué

I.

lake, river, bed, deep sea,
    mussels, scallops, snails, fortune-
plans, maps, and scrolls …

how a Sailor sails his Sea, is
    the question which has been
privy to my mind, these recent days.

    extravaganza! *prokeleumatikos!**

(vacation? yes. I need one …
    to eschew the eider ducks
from their hunting trails …)

whistle, train, farewell! put-on-attire,
     look-your-best, pack your suitcase;
you are going away now, you don't want

to tell the rest.

* Greek word

A Limerick

There was once an old Russian,
  who thought he was a Prussian;
  He traveled to Prussia,
  Finding nothing but Russia,
And he still claims to be so certain.

Sir, 'tis Past The Hour for Chatting Verse

I came to
after consenting with a bout
of cold demerits

fresh morning tide
breakfast was gallant

there were
(as I recall, in pieces,)

revolving imbroglios
past-tense superlatives
adverse conjunctions
collared crimping
jogging jests

but after all,
a clear sense of understanding

a new you (as it were)

For These

pawns of aggrandizement,
I
crown
you
       Apperceptionist …
loyal,
smooth,
unselfish.

XXX-9

There is a puff of white cloud
Over the top of that building.
It hovers flamboyant
pixyish,
teasing,
nursing the sharp edges of its edifice,
become its knight with his visor
gleaming against the naked sun.

At dawn, fresh from dreams,
I looked at the morning
and
it had rained.
Nature had poured out a benediction of moisture and rhapsody.
Creatures were climbing out of brawny branches,
Celebrating their sing-song medleys.

I, on the other hand, was spoon-feeding my soul
with the wonders of the universe

Every Weave A Thrace

"why do you let her treat you
like a child?" …the words bit me
as if they were true …

(they *were* true!)
a pound bit foolish,
feet compressed,
skies upturned,
people jumping,
skirts in sways and programmed motions.

I said,
"her personality was too strong;
it's nothing I said, or did!
uhh—I feel more powerful now
that, as opposed to my old motives,
foggy and kaleidoscopic desires,
my tastes have seamstressed …
into spring bowls, quiet dares."

After Reading Cornel Lengyel (And John Milton)

a cry so far,
so faint …

that is the illusion of a ravishing ghost:
to pour benediction on the heads of frozen cedar;
a thin rasp that strands the Milky Way to listen
to the soft perspicacious tune of the Voice within

a rapture is most embarrassing if its most inherent
feminine captive is not lighted and timbered with
fire of sacrifice over the Gordian knot, but imbroglio!
I see no task is too herculean as that of winning a flame.

and making her adore you, whether for your masculine
egotism, or your very impressionable tales
over mint juleps and milk
chocolates into the far

night.

(Cornel Lengyel was a poetry critic in Chicago.)

Rituals

rituals roost:

they fill shopping cars with merchants' green,
they dress garishly on Halloween.
they behave more or less, on cue
than a mere, "How do you do!"

the females kill with their seductions,
they emit invisible suctions;
but when you express interest in them,
they feign coy, wanting diadems.

the males, more stupid, flaunt like peacocks,
brass like bull elephants and ape jocks;
when you strike a conversation,
they assume you're gay, from a foreign nation.

rituals roost:
in businesses, presses, and plays;
the overlooked yawns in dismal obscurity days.
the habits of forces generate forces of habits
like male drakes clowning in a pond full of Playboy rabbits.

Safari

when pulled, the zebras run
with greater gamut
and the sound of their hooves
inundate

the domed craniums of the other beasts,
bar touch none *Homo erectus,*
on pulley, safari,

restless foam issues
from mouth of babes
(of baby apes)

who, by instinct or caution
pressed-on-breasts
of seasoned parents,

sniff and growl,
in dismay and pain;
scouring the trees

for shelter

Mountain Verses

Mountain verses from forever asterisks, vestibules
green emotions like poplars stand raw and unobtrusive
hidden eyewitnesses are the hews which
are aware of my ankles with the purple muslin clothing.

Dive in The Spouting Cone

Autumn, canst smell the radiant atmosphere,
whence tread palely all animals in the sphere
of dull and unpleasant Sun encumbered out
of its glory, hence the trees that stir no youth?

I could mingle with the azure world,
and steep in the fading valley of the horizon
I would sink in the murky deep cold
of the oceans and dive in this spouting cone.

O sack of winds inhaled and burst in here,
into Nature's bosom you spear:
stab the lake, hurl the cock,
and scratch at the roots of the rock.

BOOK VI

...Prose Poems

BOOK VI

PROSE POEMS

Once Again, The World

once again, the world, coiled up like a chattering monkey,
up and down flails, gnashes its teeth, shrieks savagely,
threatening to strike, swinging the bough on which he sits,
madly oscillating, shaking the apples from the tree.
we watch in despair, and talk in low whispers, wondering
what happened to our …Shangri-la, our morsel of scant
peace, which came and went, like the puff of wind it was,
trilling with oboe-laughter, the kind, in an eighteenth-

century French play; complete with marionettes and swordsmen.
tell me, Sir, will it be pistols or swords? I will fight you to
the death, and defend my honor! thrum the lute, pulse the
guitar with your thumb, brushing your lips; your tongue gilt-
edged, your hand thrusting the steel, to draw blood. the
embroidery in the clouds, somewhat dark, gloomy, forming
plump raisins of rain on Pharaoh's sarcophagus and his
armies as thick as a swarm of locusts

on the dusty plains.

Ritual for Waking

wood nymph reclines in cold December in the mountain
enjoining streams and egrets

the Sun be languid the Sun dreamy not *daring* to raise his
eyelid to come in contact his body cold the Redwoods cold

primitive and unspoiled with parcels of mythos and neglect
looking at a glance looking at Lebanon

the Jordan River my ancestral home where sightless and voiceless
people humanity converged convened and shaped a memorable
religion and took refuge in the Ark

the land of Jordan which like the land of Nagorno-Karabagh
and the lands of Armenia and Ararat regales and smites don't
forget the lands of Ur and the Hittites

so what will happen to the world. I wonder what will take
humanity to its next mythos

will the country *my* country Jordan and the heartland *my*
motherland Armenia and the city Jerusalem *my* Jerusalem

be mine again

Let's Go, My Captain

(Dedicated to Walt Whitman)

Let's go, my Captain! Let's go!
...high swells the sea foam like wool jerseys envelops the
chest and promontory on the Cape

And the Ribbon which is the Horizon, spits out dolphins
and anemones from this R. L. Stevenson Treasure Chest by
multihued magician's pulley of lime and lilac neckerchiefs

Let's go. Let's go, if we stay here, our experiences will
only be poorer all but for the wonders
Buried in Yellow Sea, Bay of Bengal, South China Sea,
adventures you told me, of
Ten eager boys, five ponies, six girls, the Sea, a mast ...

Prose-Poem Collection Entitled "Incidentally"

AMULET

In your medicine bag keep this Poem (anathema) for the rare times that you fully anticipate bouts with anxiety-related insomnia …those somersaults of sounds …from …(yecch!) neighbors …ships …pirates …troubling seas …(yuck! neighbors!)

Aromatic teas …here, sip, small caplets of sweet-smelling medicine let it …revive the tongue inner passages Corridors of Sinus (not to be confused with Cass Corridor in Detroit), the well which descends into the lagoon of the stomach, anchoring focus away from chattering Mind enamored with its e-mails

In hypnotic dosages squeeze the dropper bottle as though it were a rubber breast saddled with warm pouches of milk squeezed gently from maroon nipples sweetened with maternal love and dragoon-weary soldiers returning from Napoleonic Wars in the arms of perfumed lovers and their soft kisses …

Be philosophical and dissociate yourself from the problem as such because the mind loves to label and may be like a fox, bounding after malice like a terrier hound who knows when to be quiet but doesn't because he remains a dog

Ah, my friend, toss yourself into the Sea, let it turn itself into infinity and cinnamon cake

Weave stories with no directions with no plots so that …

the waves of Time and arms of the clock become tired with their gyrations, they go to another planet in order to bother the inhabitants there

Lemyullia and Jyeekyarra from Alpha Quadrant hMh welcome you (WELcome you, my SON!) into their distant abode because they're experienced with the sleep-deprived …

Therefore, not long ago and not long after and of many and of some, what is here and what is not and so let us tie this beastie and depart (as the old English Axiom said …)

We're passing by Marrakesh Bedouins, Baalbeck ruins shattered
Roman baths, Galapagos lizards, Swiss Choo-Choo trains
Bays and lakes, flora and fauna, vast galaxies
Immersing you as you take (the Amulet)
Dunking you into the Nekhrig Pool
Medicine pouch velvet Jersey milk from bottle accented
with luscious rainforests endowed with natural beauty

Fertile breasts fertile breasts breasts breasts unto that Valley, which, on Terra, by our calculations fifteen thousand years ago, they described in an obscure book like Shalimar, or the land of Milk and Honey.

Whatnot

I thought I loved you and I looked at you but you see you
were not a glass bottle or shale green but an ocean of magma
(fire, bubbles, gila monster) desires were evidently climbing out
from your eye sockets at the same time that your lips were saying
no and your nose imitating frightened Palomino horses and fear like
Venusian ivy with actual toes and feet
    climbing out like displaced populaces
    In riddles the object is to tease as well as to teach that is why
you were sent to me as a riddle even tho I should have first fallen
in love with your soul (blue-green)
    Instead, at forty-six you stood not an ounce trammeled with
age, or crow's feet perching on your face or eagles pecking to keep
predators away, you see, I was not a predator, I was a lover …
    could you blame me? whatnot? whatnot?

Mikken was a gentle creature; I met him in a very strange way, when I was in a distant city, in a distant land, wrapped with a mission cold and gloomy, and my eyes heavy as if bundled in pasty gum and gauze

Suddenly I remembered, and I was there and I looked at him, and I knew and a flood of memories rushed into my brain, and the storm sewer rumbled in the middle of Chopin piano and the windows jostled from that Niagara Chandelier-ice-crinkles-rain down pouring and the breeze whipping ice-caplets and mad-Russian expletives thunder, white, bleak, snow, Wind like hyenas muzzling, chortling at our cold cheeks wanting us for their next meal …

Good fat goose bumps, but I am still cold, still shivering, still feeling unprotected from the pack of wolves, the puffin out of its habitat and climate and alone, very much alone, but I have the consolation that I have known Mikken

He is my friend, and I feel this small, precious violet tract of land with brook-end glade,

My promise of laughter,

My friend, Mikken.

Train at Dusk

is lowering its arms, and blinking its red eyelids,
as if to say: no, you can't pass

train at dusk
is lowering its arms, just like an Egyptian queen,
in full regalia

train at dusk
is lowering its arms—look, it is the embodiment of two knights,
with their tourneys clashing,
fetching the smiles of their beautiful ladies,
who are blushing copiously because I saw them from the corner

*I also saw, at half past six, the train slithered through the corrupt
grassy knoll, but not without ruckus, rumble and noise ...for ...it
boomed its Beethoven horn, it didn't speak Chopin, it lowered its
arms in a stately way, to indicate to oncoming traffic that they
must indeed stop and pause, to partake of this, to drink and refresh
themselves, and blot out the stars, for they were swallowed by the
heat of early season and the seething cicadas with their incessant
behavior of spring break-boorishness.*

Boysenberry Chairs

DEAR sour belly of the aphid, I am truly sorry:
you ate the remaining candy-coconut-raisin-nougat from
the movie concession stand,
while I ate a regular meal
and I washed it down with a soothing mint tea
in order to help me to digest it.

WHILE all you had was the moisture of lice and larvae
(who unbeknownst to either of us, were busy conducting their
mitten affairs, like movie directors, dark glasses, swept hair,
bullhorn, a flair for Greta Garbo
...from turned-around Boysenberry chairs, lip-syncing Elvis'
Blue Hawaii and piercing those berries for black nectar) and
I just tippy-toed like you didn't even exist!

I AM *truly* sorry ....

Dr. Roget During Reverie

I.

I feel it is necessary for me to tell you these things—secluded,
the Moon, through the haze and brownish copse; its metal, a
    sword in its belt, slays this city, and the Impaled stumbles,
      crashing on the vines and red curtains, its lips steel
blue,   knuckles white.

And so I ask of her an interview, and plead her to ameliorate
    my anguish at the city thus fallen. In spite of this, the
      unbounded allies of my celestial orb howl and lily-
whiten the
    heavens with bolts of lightning. And so, the clouds spume and
    foam at the pewter horizon, etching light and shadow, bone and
      bread, clinking penny and hammer on the frail houses,
shops
    and boats; gradually, increasing their coil in cutting wind, when
    the jug bursts, water pours, as if benediction and power are
      being played for a second Noah. Cats are dislocated by
this   storm; children made homeless. Bears forced out of
their lairs.
    Nature's motley, either hungry or disturbed from their beds,
    slither and grapple up the wet bracken, atop thousands of trees,
    and thick undergrowth.

But I continue to nod, slipping back into dream wherein my
mind grasps at apparitions, as one grasps at straws. I have
been working a bit too hard, at words and phrases and colorful
clowns. Therefore, a small escape, a vacation, will do me a
world of good. My pulse has quickened, my breath has become
shallow, my skin gray like groat.

210

II.

The harbor recedes, and the potential rests, so does my pen.
A soft breeze insists that I accompany it. The ship's captain
smiles broadly, and the sailors look as smart as a gaggle of
geese. And I daresay that although this is not a pirate ship,
a sense of adventure courses through my veins, as if that were
true.

Nuthatch and Robin

mountain verses form forever asterisks
green emotions like poplars stand raw and unobtrusive
hidden eyewitnesses are the hewn rocks which
are aware of my ankles and their purple muslin
clothing.

Afterword
"Moods of Crickets"

One adopts an art, at times without knowing where one is going with it. Sometimes, a poem matures, sometimes it dies. The experience of letting a poem die or live is very emotional and tied in the events and up-and-down scales of life.

Some day, I hope to view all of the preceding plateaus from a plateau higher and higher still, in order to have a more mature and patient spectrum.

And going there and tasting the rough or soft spots, I hope to be grateful for all the lessons I learned, and the newer and wider paths that such adventures will open for me.

Thank you, Reader, for joining me.

—BT

Index of First Lines

Bio: Bérj Assadour Terjimanian

PART ONE:

Bérj was born September 14, 1950, in the old city of Jerusalem and is now living in the US since November 1969. By pure chance and circumstance he began writing poetry and essays because the English language and classes (including world history and religion) were generally very popular and inspiring.

It was such an age free of electronics, personal phones, and such, and the daily world was so laughably primitive that one simply could allow his or her imagination loose, primed at times by class and year-end (high-stress) comprehension — dictation, composition, and other school exams — that oddly mirrored deep fears and stresses in the young student body, yet to be secretly frowned at by most of the parents of those students, they who thought, "Babe, you have seen <u>my</u> troubles—Snookam!"

Nevertheless, one day he declared to one of his student friends, "Hey, Jack, I could <u>never</u> write poetry," a truism of public declaration that became tritely true in a short time.

Many of the poems have appeared in poetry contests and other journals, but this is the first in book form.

PART TWO:

The actual proliferation or enthusiasm for the literary arts started, in the author's mind, when his English teacher assigned an essay, homework to be written on any subject in 1964 or 1965.

Bérj wrote an essay called "A Walk in the Rain," which within a few months was preserved in posterity in a poetic version:

221

A WALK IN THE RAIN

One lonely night I stole out,
In the pitfall of the ash-night.
The air was wet, it sang aloud,
It sang aloud into my heart.

I stole down in blinding rain,
I walked, I walked, I rolled away —
Till, nothing was left of me. In pain,
My soul that pondered, sailed a-wail.

With wet blobs of lisped rain,
I wrote "A Walk in the Rain."
Winter wallowed in my bosom,
'Cause I loved it, loved it, lose 'em.

And then I saw before the pool,
My image crying in the midst of the rain.
I saw what it contained: a fool—
A fool that held the spirit in pain.

In essence, Bérj was intensely in love with English composition and essay form, from which point his fascination with writing poetry developed.